W9-CNL-138

Writing Term Papers and Reports

the text of this book is printed
on 100% recycled paper

COLLEGE OUTLINE SERIES

Writing
TERM PAPERS
and REPORTS

George Shelton Hubbell

BARNES & NOBLE BOOKS

A DIVISION OF HARPER & ROW, PUBLISHERS

New York, Evanston, San Francisco, London

©

Fourth Edition, revised, 1962
Copyright 1941, 1946, 1951, 1955, 1956, 1957, 1958, 1962

By BARNES & NOBLE, INC.

Copyright Renewed 1969

All rights reserved. No part of this book may be reproduced or utilized in any form or by any means, electronic or mechanical, including photocopying or recording, or by any information storage and retrieval system, without permission in writing from the publisher.

L. C. Catalogue Card Number: 62–15157

SBN 389 00125 2

Manufactured in the United States of America

Foreword

The purpose of this volume is two-fold. (1) It is intended to stimulate the student's interest in research methods and to help him attain the utmost enduring value from the preparation of the required documented papers. (2) It is intended to serve the undergraduate for four years as a useful desk manual, supplying suggestions for choice of subject; a step-by-step guide for the systematic gathering and preparation of material; models for footnotes and bibliographical style; and a classified, concisely annotated directory to more than three hundred standard reference works.

This book assumes that the student is actually writing a documented paper. For each of the nine steps in the task there is an assignment, and a chapter furnishing relevant information and advice. Thus learning and doing may be advanced in one operation. There is also included a specimen documented article with outline, bibliography, and footnotes arranged exactly in the form required. By referring to this article, the student may visualize the finished and integrated result of the various detailed processes.

During the preparation of the first paper, if possible, the student's work should have some inspection and criticism at each stage. Though this involves for instructors a great deal of time and planning, it is probably necessary if the project as a whole is to be very effective. Otherwise students may complete the large task before they discover that mistakes at an early stage vitiate most of what they have done. The specific directions for uniform practice here prescribed should facilitate the use of assistants and of class criticism for much of the needed checking up.

Of course the methods indicated here are not the only correct ones. They are not the best for all purposes. They have been chosen for their advantages to beginners. In later research studies a student may have to learn and use different systems. But the ability to follow one acceptable system consistently is a valuable skill. That skill may be gained from this practice. And other systems vary from this one only in certain details to which students may easily accustom themselves.

For many of the ideas in this book, the author is indebted to his colleagues in the Department of English in the University of California at Los Angeles. He is particularly grateful to Dr. Carl S. Downes for expert assistance with the proof.

The Advantages of Research

You are going to prepare a research paper. What is research? Some think of it as an almost occultly clever activity which produces the marvels of science, industry, and business. Such glorified cleverness, these people feel sure, must be far beyond the powers of an undergraduate. But others consider research a dull round of obvious observations, literal notes on the records of other observers, all written in an abominable style, with a flare of superficial statistics, and perhaps a few doubtful, trivial conclusions. Each of these opinions gives a true picture of some research. But between the two extremes there is also a modest but valuable kind of research that any student can with great profit learn to do.

Some important values may be gained by mastering the method of research. (1) Almost all vocations employ some sort of research, for skill in which a knowledge of the basic method is prerequisite. Agriculture, journalism, salesmanship, insurance, even housekeeping, bookkeeping, golf, and contract bridge may involve research. (2) Science, the learned professions, and most higher scholarship, for better or for worse, have made a fetish of research. In such work one is fairly lost without it. (3) Most important of all, the success of research in these various fields only demonstrates the real validity of the method. For many purposes it is the best way to study, the best way to think. It is, in other words, highly educational.

This validity of research as a way of study is based upon certain characteristics of the method. (1) *It is thorough*. The researcher seeks to find out about all aspects and backgrounds of his subject. He gets access to all available knowledge about it. If the task of learning so much proves too great, he limits the subject. But within the more restricted field, he still looks for all that has been contributed, using the resources of a good modern library, which helps enormously by supplying indexes, abstracts, and huge compendiums of information. Thus the researcher, when he has done his task properly, is not ignorant — as most of us without special study are bound to be — of various little points which might invalidate the conclusions reached. And even a little unit of research which a beginner can do in a few weeks, imperfect as it must be and not really thorough, has many advantages over a hit-or-miss study by an unsound method. (2) *Research is responsible.* By the system of bibliography and footnotes, it checks up on each step of progress. Any unsupported statement is challenged by the writer himself. Exaggerations, prejudices, wish thinking are likely to be detected and set right. This does not mean that imagination and individual opinion are ruled out. They are in fact used extensively in all good research. But they are checked by facts and evidence. And if the evidence does not support them, they stand apart as especially disputable matters for which the author does not presume to require acceptance. (3) *Research is a system of world-wide collaboration.* The "learned" periodicals appear at their stated intervals, making research studies simultaneously available all over the world so that this month a Japanese scholar may find the answer to a problem which an American scholar stated last month. Perhaps this collaborative feature of research accounts, more fully than any other one cause, for the phenomenal spread of modern learning, and its astonishing results in transforming man's life. Such collaboration would be greatly impaired, of course, if it were not for the system of bibliography and footnotes, which makes available everything needful to a reader who would be more than a mere reader — who would work upon the problem himself and perhaps contribute to its solution.

Even elementary research which a student can do in a month or less can be difficult, requiring all one can give of industry, patience, persistence, ingenuity, and wisdom; but sincere researchers do not find the work dull. They enjoy its constructiveness, its prospect of sound and concrete accomplishments, its growing clarity as step follows step to a logical conclusion. And even those who do not enjoy the creativeness of research for its own sake are often willing to be researchers for the sake of the results. Nor does the writing of a research paper need to be done in a flat, uninteresting style. The language may be as strong and beautiful as the content is substantial.

Table of Contents

CHAPTER   PAGE

Foreword   v

The Advantages of Research   vii

I   The Subject   1

What to Avoid in Choosing Your Subject. How to Dis-
cover the Orientation of a Subject. How to Choose a
Subject and Adapt It to Your Purposes. A Classified
List of Topics for Research Papers: Philosophy; Re-
ligion; Social Science; Philology; Science; Useful Arts;
Fine Arts; Literature; History.

II   Books and Bibliography   19

The Use of Cards in Making a Bibliography. How to
Fill Out Bibliography Cards: For a Book; For Articles
in General Reference Books; For Magazine Articles;
For Newspaper Articles; For Serial Pamphlets and
Bulletins. The Authority for Bibliographical Information. How to Collect a Bibliographical List. A List of
Reference Works Useful Chiefly for Gathering Bibliography: Encyclopedias; Periodicals; Newspapers; Public Documents; Guides for Selecting Books; Inclusive
Lists of Books; Yearbooks and Almanacs; Gazetteers
and Atlases; Philosophy, Psychology; Religion; Sociology; Philology; Science; Useful Arts; Fine Arts;
Literature; History.

III   Preliminary Evaluation of Material   61

The Problem of Evaluation. Primary and Secondary
Sources. The Writer. The Work Itself. Suggestions
for Study.

IV   Reading and Taking Notes   68

The Use of Note Cards. Kinds of Notes: Outline Notes;
Summary and Paraphrase Notes; Quotation Notes;
Commentary Notes. The Thesis and the Classification
of Notes.

V   Organization of Material 76

The Importance of Proper Methods in Research. The
Normative Method. The Experimental Method. The
Historical Method. Other Methods and Devices Inci-
dental to Research: The Case Study; The Genetic
Method; The Comparative Method; The Survey Method;
Compilation; The Questionnaire.

VI   The Outline 85

Your Method of Organizing Material Affects Your Outline. The Outline Form. The Sentence Outline. A
Specimen Outline (Boethius To-day).

VII   Writing and Documenting the Paper 91

VIII   Arrangement of the Bibliography 99

IX   Revision: The Final Form 101

        A Specimen Documented Paper 103

        Index 159

CHAPTER ONE

The Subject

Choose a subject for your research paper. Follow the directions in this chapter.

WHAT TO AVOID IN CHOOSING YOUR SUBJECT

As the first step in your research study, you will choose a subject. Here are some kinds of subjects that, for one reason or another, you will do well to avoid.

Controversial Subjects require weighing and sifting of testimony, much of which may be biased. It is hard to be objective where facts are disputed emotionally, and good research should be objective. It should not merely argue for or against something, like a lawyer's brief.

Highly Technical Subjects. A subject requiring technical knowledge, advanced study, or a good deal of experience would probably be too difficult for a beginner. The difficulty of the subject might detract from needed attention to the method.

Distasteful Subjects. Avoid subjects that seem dull or distasteful to you. There will be a good deal of work to do upon your subject when it has been chosen. If the material is unattractive to start with, it may become more so, and any reader of the finished paper is likely to share the writer's boredom.

Subjects Hard to Investigate. It is well to avoid any subject that is poorly represented among locally available books and magazines. Remember that this type of study cannot be satisfactorily done on the basis of one or two books. At least five different works should be actually used; and in some subjects, no matter how many books are consulted, it is unwise to proceed if any one much needed work is not available.

Subjects That Are Too Broad may cause much trouble. But such subjects should be limited rather than avoided. A subject may be limited in any of numerous ways. Note the progressive limitations in the following topics.

> The Novel
>
> The Novels of Dickens (limitation by person)
>
> The Early Novels of Dickens (1834-1836) (limitation by time)
>
> The Treatment of London in Dickens' Novels (limitation by place)
>
> A Study of *David Copperfield* (limiting the number of items to be covered)
>
> The Characters in *David Copperfield* (limitation to one aspect of the subject)
>
> The Main Characters in *David Copperfield*
>
> Some of the Main Characters in *David Copperfield*
>
> A Study of Mr. Micawber
>
> The Style in Mr. Micawber's Letters

Since research should do thoroughly the task which it undertakes, a writer should use a title that indicates something within his power to accomplish. Note how the second title in each of the following pairs would make the study easier. In each case a given essay might be insufficiently thorough for the first title, but entirely satisfactory for the second.

> The Motives of the Tories
>
> Some Motives of the Tories
>
> The First Winter in the Plymouth Settlement
>
> A Brief Account of the First Winter in the Plymouth Settlement
>
> Brook Farm
>
> My Opinion of the Brook Farm Experiment
>
> My High School Course
>
> A Criticism of My High School Course

The question of whether or not a given subject is too broad depends, of course, upon the time, resources, and ability of the

2

writer. It is generally wise to err on the side of undertaking too little, rather than too much. A thorough study is likely to prove bigger than one suspects before undertaking it.

Subjects That Are Too Narrow. A subject can, however, be too narrow for the purposes of some particular study. It might be as difficult to write a satisfactory paper about the left hind leg of a frog as to write one about the history of Canada. Very minute subdivisions of knowledge are often highly technical, and their bearing upon other things is not clear without a good deal of experience and thought.

Vague Subjects. It is bad to select a vague subject. At all events, it is bad to have only a vague idea regarding what does and what does not fall within the scope of the study. In such circumstances one may do much irrelevant reading and note taking, have great difficulty in planning the paper, and finally fail to achieve a clear focus. Of course a title, because of its needed brevity, may have to be vague. Thus a title may begin with the word "some":

Some Characteristics of a Small College

Some Aspects of the New Tax Bill

Such titles are vague, and the vagueness may have the advantage of piquing a reader's interest and curiosity. These titles need not impair the study which they designate. But the writer should have a clear, definite outline which will hold him to a certain course in spite of the vagueness of his title. And any writer who finds himself groping should for his own guidance set down, in one clear sentence for each, three definitions: (a) the scope of his study (just what it will include and what it will omit of the material concerned); (b) its objective (its focus, what it will maintain, what it will seek to establish); (c) its appeal (addressing, for example: readers who know nothing about the subject; readers who have some interest in the matter and are moderately well informed about it; or specialists who are very well informed). With such precautions as these, the study should be assured of its desirable precision.

3

HOW TO DISCOVER THE ORIENTATION
OF A SUBJECT

You must discover the relations between your immediate subject and its backgrounds. Thus if you study the Indians of a certain reservation, you should know something about the American Indian race, its history, distribution, divisions, characteristics, and present problems. You should have some conception of the part which Indians play in the political, economic, and social life of the country. Such information orients a subject for you, shows you where the study belongs in relation to other matters of human knowledge.

A handy guide for orientation is the library classification of subjects. This has the advantage of inclusiveness, authority, and uniformity. The Dewey decimal system is the main basis of classification in such invaluable works as the *Guide to Reference Books* (published by the American Library Association and formerly known as *Mudge's Guide to Reference Books*) and the *Standard Catalog for Public Libraries* (published by H. W. Wilson Company). Its classification is also followed more or less on most library shelves. Other common systems, such as that of the Library of Congress, under different symbols, make similar divisions of material into classes. The ten great classes in the Dewey system are, with their library numbers and some characteristic sub-classes:

000 General Works.

Periodicals, encyclopedias, government documents, bibliographies, and other works that contain material of various classes. Some reference books of this kind may well be consulted for any subject whatsoever.

100 Philosophy, psychology, anthropology, occultism, logic, ethics.

200 Religion.

Christian antiquities, the Bible and non-Christian sacred books, creeds, homiletics, hymnology, liturgy, miracles, missions, religious education, church history, denominations (Christian, non-Christian), mythology.

300 Sociology.

Government, law, race, business, commerce, finance, post office, transportation, secret societies, social work, education, popular customs, folklore, costume.

400 Philology. (Books are arranged by languages. Below are some topics under each language.)

Orthography, etymology, phonology, grammar, prosody.

500 Pure Science.

Mathematics, astronomy, physics, chemistry, geology, ethnology, biology, botany, zoölogy.

600 Useful Arts (Applied Science).

Patents, standards and materials, agriculture, medicine, home economics, industrial arts, engineering, radio, military and naval subjects, aeronautics, mining and metallurgy, manufactures, printing.

700 Fine Arts.

Architecture, furniture, ceramics, numismatics, painting, engraving, sculpture, photography, music, games and sports.

800 Literature.

Literary forms (drama, fiction, poetry, etc.), national literatures (English, French, etc.).

900 History.

Biography, genealogy, heraldry, archeology, national histories (German, Russian, etc.).

Suppose that you have decided to study and write about the topic, "Pronunciation of English in Southern Georgia." The subject, you find, comes under phonology, which is a part of philology. Looking up phonology and philology in the *Encyclopædia Britannica,* you learn what organs of speech are concerned in making the various sounds, and how the organs, and hence the sounds, are related to each other. You read too of the important part which these sounds play in the structure and development of languages. You will also find references to authoritative works on these matters, works which may prove helpful to you if you later need special information. You will learn about the *Dictionary of American English on Historical Principles* (4 volumes published during 1938-1944 by the University of Chicago Press); George P. Krapp's *The English Language in America;* H. L. Mencken's *The American Language;* John S. Kenyon's *American Pronunciation;* Hans Kurath's *American Pronunciation;* Herbert W. Horwill's *Dictionary of Modern American Usage.* Bibliographies in these works refer to many magazine studies which specialize in English as it is used in the South. Probably then, with such a background, you will be able to classify the Southern pronunciations intelligently and to discuss their causes and significance, instead of merely mentioning them. You can thus set more accurate limits on the scope of your research paper. This is a typical result of learning the orientation of a subject.

You will discover that for most important classifications in the library system there are several types of more or less specialized reference books available. Many of these are valuable or even indispensable for competent work in the subjects which they cover. Some important types of special reference books, which of course vary in value and plan for different subjects, may be broadly classified as follows:[1]

Encyclopedia. Example: Hastings' *Encyclopedia of Religion and Ethics.*

Dictionary. Example: Smith and Zurcher's *Dictionary of American Politics.*

History. Example: Garrison's *Introduction to the History of Medicine.*

Yearbook. Example: *Yearbook of the Universities of the Empire* (British).

Atlas or collection of illustrations. Examples: *World Missionary Atlas; Pageant of America* (history).

---

1 For further illustrations of these types, see Constance M. Winchell, *Guide to Reference Books* (8th ed.; Chicago: American Library Association, 1967).

Bibliography. Example: Nickles' *Geologic Literature of North America.*

Such reference books may be found by looking under the appropriate classification in the *Guide to Reference Books,* or in the *Standard Catalog for Public Libraries,* or in a good library card catalog.

HOW TO CHOOSE A SUBJECT AND ADAPT IT TO YOUR PURPOSES

Steps: (1) Select one of the following subjects, or a similar subject, for your first research study. (2) If the title as stated seems too vague or too narrow, adjust it; or at all events limit it in your own mind for your purpose. These topics are intentionally stated rather loosely, so as to leave them open to various possible interpretations and approaches. (3) Similarly, you may be able to give your topic a timely interest by focusing upon some current problem which involves the subject. The topics are not here stated in terms of contemporary discussions, because such current issues will soon yield to new ones and become out of date. The topics in their more general form, however, are of perennial interest. It is good training to seek timely expression of old problems.

A CLASSIFIED LIST OF TOPICS FOR RESEARCH PAPERS

The numbers given with these topics are the appropriate library numbers by the Dewey system. They will help in using the bibliographical list (p. 29 ff.), which is similarly numbered. They will also help in consulting such works as the *Standard Catalog for Public Libraries,* or the A.L.A. *Catalog* and *Booklist.*

100-199 PHILOSOPHY

Psychology

133   (Mental derangements, Occultism) Can Hallucinations Make History?

135   (Sleep, Dreams) Two Theories for Interpreting Dreams.

136   (Child study, Paidology, Precocity) What Becomes of Precocious Children?
137   (Temperament) Temperaments That Succeed in School.

Philosophic Systems

149   (Utilitarianism, Pragmatism, Utility) Utility as a Criterion of Value.

Logic

165   (Fallacies) Recent Fallacies in Congress.

Ethics

172   (State ethics, Duties of citizens, Patriotism) Obedience, the Soldier's Conscience.
173   (Professional ethics) Legal Defence of the Guilty.
174   (Ethics of amusements) The Spoils of College Football.
176   (Sexual ethics, Freedom of the press, Censorship) Novels That Have Been Censored.
177   (Social ethics) Duty and the Ivory Tower.
178   (Temperance, Stimulants) Undergraduate Intemperance.
179   (Morals of the press, Newspapers) Is the Undergraduate Press Free?
      (Virtues and vices) Some Deadly Virtues I Have Known.

Philosophers

184   (Social ethics, Friendship, Plato) Examples of Friendship in Plato's Dialogues.
194   (Rousseau) The Relation between Rousseau's Philosophy and His Character.

200-299 RELIGION

218   (Natural theology, Future life, Immortality) The Conception of Immortality in the ——— Religion.
245   (Hymnology, Religious poetry) Desirable Qualities in a Hymn.
257   (Parochial or parish libraries) Characteristics of a Small Church Library.

263   (Sunday observance) An Ideal Use of Sunday.

264   (Public worship, Divine service, Ritual, Liturgy) Desirable Features of Public Worship in ———— Church.

267.311   (Religious societies of men, Y. M. C. A.) The Most Needed Improvement in the Y. M. C. A.

272.8   (Persecution of witches. See also 133.4, Witchcraft) Evidences of Sincerity in the Salem Witch-Burners.

292   (Greek and Roman mythology) Symbolism in the Greek Worship of Demeter.

298   (Mormonism. See also 173.2, Polygamy) Present-Day Polygamy among the Mormons.

300-399 SOCIAL SCIENCE

Political Science

324.275   (Voting, Miscount of ballots) A Case of Fraud in Counting Votes.

328.334   (Legislation, Representation) What Do My State's Representatives Represent?

329   (Political parties) Some Present Weaknesses in the ———— Political Party.

Economics

331.2   (Wages, Hire, Pay, Salary, Fees) Economic Status of the Wage Earner in ————.

331.89   (Strikes) The Government's Attitude toward Strikes in ————.

332   (Money, Credit. See also 378.36, Student loan funds) Disadvantages of Student Loans.

336.24   (Income tax) Some Methods of Evading the Income Tax.

Law

343.1   (Criminal trials) "Fixed" Juries in Three Famous Trials.

343.2   (Criminal law, Punishments) Theory and Experience with the Baumes Law.

347.94   (Evidence) Reliability of Evidence by Experts.

Administration

351.3   (Civil service examinations) Several Abuses of the Federal Civil Service.

352   (City government) Recent Reforms in the Government of ―――― City.

355.4   (Military tactics, Strategy) Tactics Employed in the Battle of ――――.

Institutions

362   (Hospitals) How a Modern Hospital Is Organized.

365   (Prisons) Abuses of Parole in ――――.

Education

371.27 (Examinations) Practices That Diminish the Value of Examinations.

371.37 (Seminary method of instruction) Advantages of the Seminary Method.

371.595 (School city) How Some School Cities Have Worked.

371.733 (School military drill) Characteristics of Compulsory Military Training in ――――.

371.945 (Precocity in education) Some Precocious Students and How They Turned Out.

372.1   (Nursery schools) What a Nursery School May Do for a Child.

372.6   (Arithmetic) How ―――― Teaches Arithmetic Effectively.

373   (Secondary education) Why Some Students Have Not Learned How to Study before They Enter College.

374.1   (Conversation) Why Not Teach Conversation?

376   (Education of women) The Educational Needs of a Modern American Girl.

378.153 (City vs. country colleges) Advantages of a Rural College Campus.

378.99 (Professional and technical education) Disadvantages of an Early Start in Technical Education.

379.12 (State and federal aid to schools) Strings Tied to School Funds from the Government of ———.

379.3 (Private, endowed schools) Advantages of a Private School.

Trade, Communication, Transportation

381 (Domestic trade) Costs of Competition in the ——— Trade (in the U. S.).

382 (Foreign trade) Effects of the Tariff on the ——— Trade.

384 (Telephone) If the Postal Department Operated the Telephone Service.

385 (Railroad) Will Railroads Become Obsolete?

400-499 PHILOLOGY

408 (Universal language) Why Not Esperanto?

421.4 (Spelling reform) Advantages of a Proposed Spelling Reform.

426 (Prosody, Sonnet) The Mechanical Structure of a Sonnet.

427 (Dialects) Characteristics of Spoken English in ———.

430-490 (Various foreign languages) A Good Way to Learn the ——— Language.

470 (Latin) How Latin Helps in English.

500-599 SCIENCE

Mathematics

510 (Mathematics) The Function of Mathematics in the ——— Process.

511 (Arithmetic, Graphs) Why Some Graphs Are Misleading.

Astronomy

520 (Astronomy) Astronomy in the Poetry of ———.

522.2 (Telescopes) Structure and Function of the ——— Telescope.

11

523.43   (Mars) What Is It Like on Mars?

523.5   (Meteors) Meteors Found in ———.

523.78   (Eclipses) The Eclipse of the Sun in ———.

523.8   (Stars) How the ——— Stars Were Discovered and
          Classified.

527   (Navigation) Skills a Navigator Needs.

Physics

532   (Hydrostatics, Hydraulics) Some Efforts to Utilize Tidal
          Power.

534.8   (Acoustics) Some Influences of Acoustics upon Archi-
          tecture.

535.84   (Optics, Spectroscopy, Spectrum analysis) Some Con-
          quests by Spectroscope.

536.83   (Heat, Ventilation, Air conditioning. See also 697, Build-
          ings) One Type of Air Conditioning.

537   (Electricity. See also 640, Domestic economy) Some
          Applications of Electricity in the Kitchen.

Chemistry

540   (Chemistry) What a Child Can Learn with a Small
          Chemistry Set.

540   (Applied chemistry) Some Synthetic Materials Newly in
          Use.

546.432   (Radium) Dangers in Using Radium.

Geology

551.5   (Meteorology, Weather, Aviation) The Part of Meteor-
          ologists in Aviation.

553.5   (Economic geology, Building stones) Building Stones
          from the State of ———.

553.8   (Mineralogy, Gems, Precious stones) The Finding and
          Marketing of Rubies.

568   (Paleontology. See also 571, Fossils) Fossil Animals
          Found in the State of ———.

Biology

571.7   (Prehistoric archeology, Rudiments of art) Some Artifacts Found in the Ruins of ———.

572.4   (Ethnology, Anthropology) Was ——— the Original Home of Man?

579.1   (Skeletons, Anatomy) How to Assemble the Skeleton of a ———.

Botany

581.23   (Plant pathology, Parasites) Parasites to Control Parasites on ——— Plants.

581.5   (Plant habits) Wild Plants That Distinguish Good Farming Land.

583   (Trees, Herbs, Flowers, Shrubs) How to Raise ——— Plants.

Zoölogy

597.8   (Toads, Frogs) The Feeding Habits of Frogs and Toads.

598.20   (Birds) Habits of a Familiar Bird.

599.30   (Rodents, Rats, Mice) Some Laboratory Uses of Rodents.

599.5   (Cetacea, Whales) Tendencies in Modern Whaling.

600-699 USEFUL ARTS

Medicine

612.3942 (Food, Babies. See also 613.22, Food for infants) Recent Tendencies in the Feeding of Babies.

613.51   (Sanitation) Some Recent Advances in Sanitary Housing.

614.2   (State control of medicine) The Present Extent of State Control of Medicine.

614.3   (Pure food laws) Some Needed Reforms in the Pure Food Laws.

614.5   (Contagious and infectious diseases) Recent Improvements in Public Control of ——— Disease.

616.12   (Heart) Causes and Some Treatments of Heart Disease.

617.95   (Plastic surgery) Some Recent Achievements of Plastic Surgery.

Engineering

621.434 (Diesel engines) Some Difficulties in the Adaptation of Diesel Engines.

622.5 (Drainage of mines) Some ·Problems in the Drainage of Mines.

623.55 (Gunnery, Ballistics) Sighting and Firing of Modern Siege Guns.

624.5 (Suspension bridges) Some Engineering Methods in the Construction of ———— Bridge.

626 (Canal engineering) Some Engineering Devices in the Operation of the ———— Canal.

629.13 (Aeronautics) Some Mechanical Faults of Aircraft in 1917.

629.155 (Dirigible airships) Some Engineering Improvements in Recent Dirigibles.

Agriculture

631.8471 (Nitrogen fertilizers) Some Modern Uses of Nitrifying Crops.

633 (Grains, Cereals, Fibers) Some of the Risks in Growing Wheat (Rye, Oats, Corn, Cotton).

634 (Fruits, Orchards) Navel Orange [Grapefruit, Avocado] Culture in the United States.

636.4 (Pigs, Swine) Qualities for Which Pigs Are Bred.

Domestic Economy

641 (Food values) Essentials in a Well Balanced Meal.

643.33 (Stoves) The Ideal Kitchen Range.

645 (Furniture, Carpets, Upholstery Decoration) Points to Consider in Furnishing a Room.

647.1 (Household budget) A Simple Domestic Budget.

Commercial Arts

651 (Business secretarial work) Qualifications of a Good Office Secretary.

655.28 (Typesetting, Linotype) Advantages and Limitations of the Linotype.

Manufactures

674 (Wood turning, Lathes) Uses and Limitations of Wood-turning Lathes.

Buildings

693.8 (Fireproofing) What Can Make a Building Fireproof?

700-799 FINE ARTS

Landscape Gardening

715 (Shrubs) The Right Shrub in the Right Place.

Architecture

721 (Architectural construction, Materials) Some New Building Materials That Make Possible New Designs.

727.3 (Educational architecture) What Style of Architecture Is Most Suitable for a Modern University?

728 (Residences) Some Very New Ideas in Domestic Architecture.

Sculpture

731 (Materials and methods in sculpture) How a Statue Is Made.

Drawing

742 (Perspective) How an Artist Obtains Perspective.

Painting

759.2 (Reynolds) Characteristics of Portraits by Sir Joshua Reynolds.

Engraving

761 (Wood engraving, Woodcuts) Some Special Advantages of Woodcuts for Book Illustrations.

Photography

770 (Photographic illustrations) Artistic Principles in Recent Books and Magazines of Pictures.

778 (Cinema, Moving pictures) Efforts to Get Subjective Effects in Moving Pictures.

Music

782.6 (Comic opera, Gilbert and Sullivan) Some Comic Elements in the Gilbert and Sullivan Operas.

783.8 (Sacred music, Boys' choir) Value of the Training in a Boys' Choir.

785.1 (Orchestral music, Symphony) How to Appreciate a Symphony Concert.

786-789 (Instruments) Requirements and Opportunities for Players of the ———.

Amusements

794-799 (Games, Chess, etc.) Some Promising Contenders for the Championship in Chess (Billiards, Bowling, Tennis, Golf, Boxing, Baseball, etc.).

796 (Football, etc.) The Prospects for a Career in Professional Football (Baseball, Tennis, Golf, etc.).

799 (Angling, Trout) Some Fine Points in Casting for Trout.

800-899 LITERATURE

811.32 (American poetry, Poe) How Poe Applied His Theory of Poetry in His Poems. (This topic can be used for most poets who have stated their theory of poetic composition: e.g., Sidney, Jonson, Dryden, Pope, Wordsworth, Shelley, Arnold, Emerson, Amy Lowell, etc.)

812.5 (O'Neill) Some Technical Experiments of Eugene O'Neill and Their Effect.

813.45 (American short stories, Harte) Local Conditions and Characters in the Stories of Bret Harte. (This general topic may be used for such writers as: Hamlin Garland, Hawthorne, O. Henry, Joel Chandler Harris, etc.)

821.3 (Shakespeare's sonnets) The Story behind Shakespeare's Sonnet Series. (The general topic will serve for sonnet series by Sidney, Spenser, Wordsworth, Mrs. Browning, Rossetti.)

821.78 (Keats) Fanny Brawne and the Poetry of Keats. (The influence of some lady upon a poet's work often makes a promising subject. See the poetry of Dante, Alfred de

Musset, Goethe, Sidney, Spenser, Herrick, Cowper, Burns, Wordsworth, Byron, Shelley, Keats, Browning, etc.)

822.3 (Elizabethan dramatic companies) Boys as Elizabethan Actors.

822.33 (Shakespeare's *Othello*) The Structure of *Othello* as a Typical Tragedy.

822.91 (Bernard Shaw) Some Social Purposes in Shaw's Plays and How They Are Served.

823.83 (Dickens) Some Social Conditions Which Dickens Assailed in His Novels.

823.91 (H. G. Wells) Some Prophecies of H. G. Wells.

831.75 (Heine) Autobiographical Elements in Some of Heine's Poems.

832.62 (Goethe) How Gounod's Opera Modifies Goethe's *Faust*.

839.8364 (Hans Christian Andersen) Was Hans Christian Andersen the Ugly Duckling?

841.45 (La Fontaine) The Main Aspects of Humanity as Shown in La Fontaine's Fables.

843.76 (Alexandre Dumas, the elder) What Makes a Dumas Romance Exciting.

844.31 (Montaigne) The Traits of a Typical Essayist, as Seen in Montaigne.

851.15 (Dante) An Account of Dante's Beatrice.

851.18 (Petrarch) An Account of Petrarch's Laura.

863.32 (Cervantes) What Is Satirized in *Don Quixote?*

871.2 (Ovid) Interpretations of One of Ovid's Myths.

873.1 (Virgil) Some Roman History in Virgil's Underworld.

875.1 (Cicero) Did Cicero Misrepresent Catiline?

882.1 (Aeschylus) The *Agamemnon* as a Typical Greek Play.

883.1 (Homer) What Was Heroic in Achilles?

883.3 (Xenophon, Plato) Socrates in the *Memorabilia* Compared with Socrates in the *Symposium*.

900-999 HISTORY
Travels

915 (Marco Polo) Some Probable Facts in Marco Polo's Travels.

916.7   (Henry M. Stanley) The Africa Which Stanley Penetrated.

Biography

920   (Samuel Pepys) How the Pepys Diary Illustrates Some Prominent People of the Day.

929.2   (Henry Adams) Why Have the Later Adamses Held Few Electoral Offices?

931   (Confucius) The Main Abuses Attacked by Confucius.

History

932   (Egypt) How the History of Ancient Egypt Has Been Revealed in Modern Times.

937   (Rome) Amenities of Court Life under Augustus.

938   (Greece) In Defence of Alcibiades.

940.1   (Medieval Europe) A Day in a Medieval Village.

940.2   (Modern Europe) A Day in a Medici Palace.

940.3   (European War, 1914-1918) What Drew America into the War?

940.5   (Later 20th century. See also 323, 445, Freedom of the Press) Development of Press Censorship in ———— since 1918.

942.04   (English history, 1399-1485) Have Historians Been Unfair to Richard III?

944.04   (French Revolution) What the Popular Leaders Hoped from the French Revolution.

947.084 (Russian Revolution, 1917) Trotsky's Role at the Beginning of the Revolution.

951   (China) Some Preliminary Labors of Dr. Sun-Yat-Sen.

973.7   (U. S. Civil War) Diplomacy in England during the Civil War.

973.8   (Later 19th century in the U. S.) Some Social Consequences of the Exploitation of One Natural Resource during This Period.

CHAPTER TWO

Books and Bibliography

Make a preliminary working bibliography of your subject. Follow the directions in this chapter.

THE USE OF CARDS IN MAKING A BIBLIOGRAPHY

Before starting the search for library material on your subject, you must learn how to make a bibliography and how to take reading notes.

Bibliographies are made and kept on cards. The ordinary cards for this purpose are three by five inches. Some students like larger ones, affording more space for comments about the books. Some prefer uniform slips of paper, because they are cheaper, easier to carry, and perhaps easier to use in a typewriter. But at all events it is desirable that you should select the kind of cards or slips which you prefer, and use that kind consistently hereafter whenever you have occasion to record bibliographical items. Carry the materials always, and keep all your bibliography cards filed systematically and permanently. This habit will prove most valuable, in more ways than you can foresee at present.

A card should contain the bibliographical reference for only one book or article. This is very important. You can see that the material cannot be rearranged or filed effectively if several items are placed on a single card. One item may occupy several cards, however. There may be a temptation to save expense and trouble by putting several references in a list on one card or on an odd slip of paper, especially if there seems slight chance that they will be important in your study. But such economies are costly in the long run. The development of good bibliographical habits is well

19

worth the cost of cards. And if you really cannot afford to buy new cards, it may be possible to obtain free some cards which have been used on one side.

It is important to follow a uniform practice in filling out bibliography cards. You will find that the title pages, library cards, and various lists of books use different systems. Title pages give little or no punctuation; and, since most of the material there is printed in capitals, you get no help from a title page regarding capitalization. Neither do library cards help in that matter of capitalizing. As for bibliographical lists, each one follows its own system, with abbreviations and punctuation adapted to its peculiar purposes. In the *Cumulative Book Index*,[1] for example, a colon after the initial J means that the name abbreviated is John. This valuable work also abbreviates the names of publishing houses to a word or so, sending the reader to a list at the end of the volume for the full name and exact address. But you are not to follow any of these methods. You should feel that what you write on your card is your master record for the book or article under consideration. It may serve not only for the present study, but for future reference as well. Therefore you must have your card legible, accurate, complete, sparing in abbreviations, punctuated by your own consistent system. Others besides yourself should be able to use it. There should be no need for further reference to the volume itself to verify or complete the entry. Care and time for the making of such a card are well spent.

Your bibliography as given with your finished research paper will probably contain only the conventional information for each reference. It is a good practice, however, to add at the bottom of the card or on the back, for your own use, various further matters that come to your attention. Thus you might, if you are interested, note the price of the book, the presence of bibliographies, illustrations, or indexes, the location and gist of reviews. And when you are reading a book, you may want to note on its card any special

---

1 This publication lists all books published in English.

emphasis or omissions, inaccuracies, adaptability to certain purposes, apparent bias, etc. But of course a bibliography can hardly serve as a substitute for reading notes.

HOW TO FILL OUT BIBLIOGRAPHY CARDS

For a Book.

What to Put Down.

AUTHOR. Put down the last name first, followed by a comma, then the other names just as you find them, followed by a period. Example: Beer, Thomas.

TITLE. Put down the title exactly and completely as you find it, but capitalize the important words (first word, last word, all emphatic words, all other words except articles, conjunctions, and prepositions), underline the whole title (a printer italicizes it), and follow it by a period. Do not change the spelling or abbreviate any words that you find spelled out. You may omit a subtitle. Example: *The Mauve Decade.*

FACTS OF PUBLICATION. Give: place of publication, followed by a colon; name of the publisher, followed by a comma; date of publication ("n.d.," if no date appears), followed by a period Example: New York: Alfred A. Knopf, Inc., 1942.

A whole reference: de Grazia, Alfred. *Public and Republic.* New York: Alfred A. Knopf, Inc., 1951.

A Simple Case. Let us suppose that you want to make a card for Robinson's *The Mind in the Making.* Here is an entry which you find in the *Cumulative Book Index.*

Robinson, James Harvey, 1863 ——
  Mind in the making; the relation of intelligence to social reform.
  New ed 0 235p $1 '30 Harper

Here is what you find on the title page of the book:

THE

MIND IN THE MAKING

*The Relation of Intelligence
to Social Reform*

By

JAMES HARVEY ROBINSON

Author of
*PETRARCH, THE FIRST MODERN SCHOLAR
MEDIAEVAL AND MODERN TIMES
THE NEW HISTORY*, ETC.

HARPER & BROTHERS PUBLISHERS
NEW YORK AND LONDON

Here is what you find on the Library of Congress card in your library card index, under the author's name.

301　Robinson, James Harvey, 1863—

The mind in the making; the relation of intelligence to social reform, by James Harvey Robinson . . . New York and London, Harper & brothers (°1921)

　　5 p. 1.(3)—235p. 21½ᶜᵐ.

"Some suggestions in regard to reading": p. (231)—235.

—— —— Copies 2-5.

1. Social psychology. 2. Civilization—Hist. 3. Social problems. I. Title. Official.

21-20447

Library of Congress　　　　HM251.R73
—— —— Copy 2.

Copyright A627806　　　　　　(s22f5)

You can fill out your card from any one of these sources, but in any case you will omit some of the material, and you will use your own arrangement and punctuation. Your result will probably be:

> Robinson, James Harvey. <u>The</u> <u>Mind</u> <u>in</u> <u>the</u> <u>Making.</u> New York and London: Harper and Brothers, n.d.

But some variations are possible in this. You might choose to use the subtitle. You might follow the library card, with its date in parentheses. The parentheses indicate, however, that the date does not appear on the title page. As a matter of fact, it is the date of the copyright and may or may not be the date of the first edition. Or you may follow the *Cumulative Book Index* by giving the date as 1930, which is the date of a later edition. Also, if you follow this source, you will omit the article as the first word of the title. What you do about such details is not a matter of indifference. A misleading date, for instance, might introduce a serious fault into your paper. Perhaps you would do well to add a note on your card, such as: "Copyright date, 1921. The edition used is of 1930." You may consider such scrupulousness fussy. It is largely this kind of care that makes the scientific method trustworthy and effective. Whenever you make out a card on the basis of the data in some list, and then proceed to consult the book, check the material on your card to see whether it corresponds with the title page. If the date or anything about the actual book is different, change your card so that all the information listed will be completely accurate and up-to-date. Your card must represent the very edition you have used; if it does not represent the same edition, it may prove misleading.

Books That Require Special Attention.

Two or Three Authors.

Auslander, Joseph and Hill, Frank Ernest. *The Winged Horse.* Garden City, N. Y.: Doubleday, Doran and Company, 1929.

More than Three Authors.

Canby, Henry Seidel and others. *English Composition in Theory and Practice.* New York: The Macmillan Company, 1909.

No Author Named.

Books Printed by Aldus Manutius and His Successors. Leipzig: Gustav Fock, 1935.

An Edited Text.

Spenser, Edmund. *The Fowre Hymnes.* Edited by Lilian Winstanley. Cambridge: Cambridge University Press, 1916.

A Numbered Edition.

Bartlett, John. *Familiar Quotations.* Seventh edition. Boston: Little, Brown and Company, 1878.

A Revised Edition.

Manly, John Matthews and Rickert, Edith. *Contemporary American Literature.* Introduction and revision by Fred B. Millett. New York: Harcourt, Brace and Company, n.d.

Issued by a Board or Committee as Author.

College Entrance Examination Board. *Questions Set at the Comprehensive Examinations of 1920.* Boston: Ginn and Company, n.d.

An Anthology.

Thomas, C. W., editor. *Essays in Contemporary Civilization.* New York: The Macmillan Company, 1931.

When Only One Volume of a Set Is Used.

Taylor, Henry Osborn. *The Mediaeval Mind.* Third (American) edition. New York: The Macmillan Company, 1919. Vol. 1.

When a Complete Set Is Used.

Mansfield, Katherine. *The Letters of Katherine Mansfield.* Edited by J. Middleton Murry. New York: Alfred A. Knopf, 1929. 2 vols.

A Book in a Series.

Wylie, Elinor. *Jennifer Lorn.* Garden City Publishing Company, n.d. (The Sun Dial Library.)

A Translation.

Brunetière, Ferdinand. *Manual of the History of French Literature.* Translated by Ralph Derechef. New York: Thomas Y. Crowell and Company, n.d.

For Articles in General Reference Books.

A Signed Article in an Encyclopedia.

AUTHOR. Enter the name and punctuate it just as for a book. In some reference works, articles are initialed, and the initials are explained at the beginning of the volume.

TITLE. The title is to be capitalized and punctuated as in the case of books. But it is not to be underlined (italicized). Instead, it is to be enclosed in quotation marks.

THE NAME OF THE REFERENCE WORK, underlined for italics, and followed by the edition and year, the volume (in arabic numerals), and the page numbers (inclusive). These items are to be separated by commas and followed by a period.

Example:

Morris, Edward Parmelee. "The Latin Language." *The Encyclopedia Americana,* 1936 edition, vol. 17, pp. 47-48.

An Unsigned Article in an Encyclopedia. Example:

Encyclopaedia Britannica, 14th edition (1929), vol. 11, pp. 616-617. Article, "Hockey."

An Article in a Reference Book Written Entirely by One Author. Example:

Newman, Ernest. *Stories of the Great Operas.* Garden City, N. Y.: Garden City Publishing Company, n.d. Vol. 2, pp. 3-44, "The Life of Mozart."

A Signed Article in a Collection or Anthology.

Davidson, Donald. "Federal Disunion; The Political Economy of Regionalism." In: Johnson, A. Theodore and Tate, Allen. *America through the Essay.* New York: Oxford University Press, 1938. Pp. 149-171.

For Magazine Articles.

AUTHOR. Put down the name as in the case of a book.

TITLE. Enter and punctuate the title as in the case of a book. But do not underline for italics; enclose the title in quotation marks.

FACTS OF PUBLICATION. Give: the name of the magazine (underlined for italics); the volume (in arabic numerals); the inclusive page numbers for the article; the date (in parentheses). These items should be separated by commas (except before the parentheses), with a period at the end.

Example:

Smart, George K. "Private Libraries in Colonial Virginia." *American Literature,* vol. 10, pp. 24-52 (March, 1938).

Notice that each number is identified by a label.

A Simple Case. Suppose that you have found the following entry in the *International Index to Periodicals.*

> SCHÜTZE, Martin
> Toward a modern humanism. PMLA 51: 284-99
> Mr '36.

Here are abbreviations that need expansion and numbers that need labeling. The *International Index* (and other books like it) explains, somewhere in each volume, its abbreviations and system of reference. Expanding them, interpreting, and using your own system, you will write the following item.

Schütze, Martin. "Toward a Modern Humanism." *Publications of the Modern Language Association of America,* vol. 51, pp. 284-299 (March, 1936).

Special Cases.

AN UNSIGNED ARTICLE

"The Federal Arts Bill." *The Saturday Review of Literature,* vol. 18, p. 8 (June 4, 1938).

A SIGNED BOOK REVIEW

Shores, Louis. Review of *Webster's Student Dictionary.* In: *Wilson Bulletin for Librarians,* vol. 12, p. 658 (June, 1938).

AN UNSIGNED BOOK REVIEW

Review of Marjorie Patten's *The Arts Workshop of Rural America.* In: *The New York Times Book Review,* vol. 43, p. 21 (June 5, 1938).

For Newspaper Articles.

What to Put Down.

The author's name, as usual. If the article is unsigned, begin with the title.

The title, as for a magazine article, in quotation marks. If there is no title, a brief title should be supplied, in square brackets.

Name of the paper, exact date, section (if necessary), page, column.

A Simple Case. You find the following entry in the *New York Times Index,* for 1936.

> Toscanini, Arturo
> Will conduct the opening concert of Palestine Symphony Orchestra, F 23, II & III, 1 :, 6

This material will appear on your bibliography card in the following form.

> "Arturo Toscanini Will Conduct the Opening Concert of Palestine Symphony Orchestra." New York Times, February 23, 1936, secs. 2 and 3, p. 1, col. 6.

For Pamphlets, Bulletins, Etc., Issued Serially by Some Person or Institution.

What to Put Down. (Punctuate as in the example below.)

For a signed publication, the author's name, as usual. If a committee or some other group has credit for the composition, the name of that group should stand as author.

The title, in quotation marks as for a magazine article.

The name of the person or institution (such as: school, department of government, business concern, church, library, etc.) which issues the publication, followed by all necessary information regarding volume, number, series, pages, place, publisher, date. Publications issued in series are like magazines in not requiring a statement of the place of publication.

A Signed Government Publication.

As listed in the *Educational Index.*

> Segel, David. Prediction of success in college; a
> handbook for administrators and investigators con-
> cerned with the problems of college admittance or
> guidance of college students. (U. S. Office of ed.
> Bul. 1934, no. 15) 98 p. bibliog pa 10c Supt. of doc.
> '34.

As listed in the *Monthly Catalog of Public Documents,* 1918, under
Interior Department, Education Office.

> Prediction of success in college, a handbook for
> administrators and investigators concerned with the
> problems of college admittance or guidance of college
> students (with bibliography) ; by David Segel. 1934.
> vii 98 p. il. 1 pl. (Bulletin 15, 1934.) *Paper, 10c

As expanded and arranged for a bibliography card.

> Segel, David. "Prediction of Success in
> College; A Handbook for Administrators
> and Investigators Concerned with the
> Problems of College Admittance or Guid-
> ance of College Students." Bulletin,
> 1934, no. 15. United States Department
> of the Interior, Office of Education.

An Unsigned Government Publication.

> "Monthly Record of Current Educational
> Publications." Bulletin, 1918, no. 12.
> United States Department of the Interior,
> Bureau of Education.

A Publication Issued by a Society.

> Morrison, Hugh Alexander. "Bibliography
> of the Official Publications of the Con-
> federate States." In: Bibliographical
> Society of America, Proceedings, 3
> (1909), pp. 92-132.

28

A Publication with an Institution as Author.

New York Public Library. "List of
Works Relating to City Charters, Ordi-
nances and Collected Documents." New
York Public Library <u>Bulletins</u> 16-17
(1912-1913).

THE AUTHORITY FOR BIBLIOGRAPHICAL INFORMATION

The final source of bibliographical information is the book
itself which you would describe. Though you may copy the desired
data from library cards or from lists, you should always, if possible, verify every detail from the title page of the book. Such
verification is desirable for many reasons. The list where you
first discover the material may be inaccurate. The actual book
that you use may be a different edition from that described in the
list; the paging, the contents, the publisher may be different.

Secondary sources of bibliographical data, such as the *United
States Catalog of Books in Print* or the *International Index to
Periodicals,* should not appear as items in the bibliography which
accompanies your essay. Such books and lists are used merely as
means for finding other works. Copy the necessary material from
the list on to your card. Then note elsewhere on the card, briefly
but clearly, for your own information, the source of the data.
As soon as you find the book or periodical itself, verify the material
on the card, and draw a line through your note regarding the
secondary source, for now you have the authority of the primary
source of such information.

HOW TO COLLECT A BIBLIOGRAPHICAL LIST

Unless you work methodically, your bibliography may become unbalanced, incomplete, or vitiated by inferior material. The
following brief list of reference works in English furnishes the
means for putting many resources of a library at your command.
To use the list properly, take these steps, in order. (1) Consult

first a good encyclopedia. Read the articles which concern your subject. Use the index volume if the encyclopedia has one. Take down any bibliographical suggestions the articles supply, for they are the recommendations of experts. (2) Turn next to the periodical indexes (pp. 32-33) and select such articles as seem most promising. Notice the date of the articles, their length, their probable relevance for your purpose, whether or not they are available in your library. Save yourself the labor of copying unavailable or merely popular titles. Do not look up the articles yet. (3) Next try newspaper indexes (p. 33-34), if your subject is one that has made news. The main thing to discover at this stage is whether or not newspapers do offer some help. If so, note the fact, but do not now take down a long list of references. (4) Look in the *Standard Catalog for Public Libraries,* finding your subject by the library classification. This will give you an excellent list of books. The *A.L.A. Booklist* or the *Book Review Digest* may be of service by indicating what the books are about, how they are to be used, and what standing they have among experts. Check the titles you select, to see whether they are available in your library.

When you have taken these four steps, you should have a fairly well balanced list of titles. Your next move will depend upon your subject and your purpose. Public documents, atlases, and yearbooks may or may not be helpful in your particular study. But turn to the reference books in your special field, using those suggested in the following list, or possibly the much fuller list in the *Guide to Reference Books.* You may find some of these works too advanced, specialized, or technical, especially if your subject is scientific. But make cards for the books that you may be able to use from such lists, and plan to consult them after you have acquired some mastery of the more general works.

A LIST OF REFERENCE WORKS USEFUL CHIEFLY FOR GATHERING BIBLIOGRAPHY

Of the two divisions in this list, the first, containing general works, is much the more useful to a beginner. The second division, of works on special fields, should be consulted only after you have made use of the more general reference tools. Many of the best specialized works, being highly technical or written in foreign languages, are omitted from this list.

FIRST DIVISION

Library Number 000

General Works, Not Limited to Any Particular Field

ENCYCLOPEDIAS

Catholic Encylopedia. 16 vols. and Supplement. New York: Catholic Encyclopedia Press, 1907-1922. Reprinted with Supplement II by Gilmary, New York, 1955.

Excellent for any subjects relating to the Catholic Church.

Chambers' Encyclopedia. 15 vols. New York: Oxford University Press, new edition, 1950.

Collier's Encyclopedia. 24 vols. New York: P. F. Collier and Son, 1968.

Columbia Encyclopedia. New York: Columbia University Press, 3rd edition, 1963.

A comprehensive single volume.

Encyclopedia Americana. 30 vols. New York and Chicago: Americana Corporation. Plate revisions annually. *Americana Annual* (1923 to date) is an annual supplement.

Contains summaries of famous books and texts of important documents. Lists of references follow many of the articles. Important articles are by specialists and are signed. Arrangement is by short articles under separate headings.

Encyclopaedia Britannica. London and New York: Encyclopaedia Britannica. 11th edition, 29 vols., 1911. Revised annually. 24 vols., 1968. *Britannica Book of the Year* (1937 to date) issued annually.

Since the alphabetical arrangement is to a large extent by general rather than by specific subjects, one should look first in the last volume, in the general index. Bibliographies follow important articles. The last volume contains an atlas.

Jewish Encyclopedia. 12 vols. New York: Funk and Wagnalls Company, 1901-1906.

Valuable for biographies and Talmudic law.

The New International Encyclopaedia. New York: Dodd, Mead and Company. 2nd edition, 23 vols., 1914-1916; Supplement, 2 vols., 1925; Supplement, 2 vols., 1930.

Universal Jewish Encyclopedia. 10 vols. New York: Universal Jewish Encyclopedia Company, 1939-1944.

PERIODICALS

Finding Periodicals.

It may happen that some articles mentioned in an index are in periodicals not kept by the library you use. The following reference work will help you to find out which libraries have the periodical.

New Series Titles; a union list of serials newly received by North American libraries, prepared under the sponsorship of the Joint Committee on the Union List of Serials. Vol. 1, no. 1, January, 1953. Washington, D.C., Library of Congress. 1953 to date.

Monthly issues with annual cumulations. This publication supersedes the *Union List of Serials in Libraries of the United States and Canada.* New York: H. W. Wilson Company, 2nd edition, 1943, includes titles through 1940. Supplements, 1941-1943, 1944-1949.

Periodical Indexes.

Some specialized indexes also cover pamphlets, bulletins, government publications, and appropriate books. Cumulative indexes reprint their separate titles periodically under one alphabet. For example, the March number of the *Reader's Guide* contains in one alphabetical arrangement all the entries which have appeared previously in the January and February numbers. In the periodical indexes, magazines are generally referred to by abbreviations, an explanation of which is found in a list printed at the front of each volume.

To 1906.

Poole's Index to Periodical Literature. Boston, Mass.: Houghton Mifflin Company, 1891. Supplements, 1907. No longer published.

Dates covered: 1802-1906. Field: 470 American and English periodicals of the 19th century. Arrangement: subject and title (not author) in one alphabet. Data: title, author, periodical, volume, page. A table shows year dates for each volume indexed.

Popular Periodicals after 1900.

Reader's Guide to Periodical Literature. New York: H. W. Wilson
Company, 1900 to date.

Monthly numbers cumulated quarterly and annually. Field: over 100
general nontechnical periodicals, the exact list changing somewhat from
year to year. Arrangement: subject, author, title, in one alphabet. Data:
title, author, periodical, volume, pages, exact date. Illustrations indicated.

General and Learned Periodicals after 1907.

International Index to Periodicals. New York: H. W. Wilson
Company, 1907 to date. (1907-1919, called *Reader's Guide to
Periodical Literature;* Supplement.)

Monthly numbers cumulated during the year and annually. Field: Social
sciences and humanities. Does not duplicate the *Reader's Guide*. (Since
1952 changes have been made in the coverage of both Indexes; a number
of titles have been transferred and others dropped.) Data: title, author,
periodical, volume, pages, date. Illustrations indicated.

Subject Indexes.

Annual Magazine Subject Index. Boston, Mass.: F. W. Faxon
Company, 1908-1952.

Vol. 1, entitled *Magazine Subject Index*, indexes some periodicals from
their first number. Field: many less familiar American and English periodicals. Does not duplicate the *Reader's Guide*. Arrangement: alphabetical by
subject, except for the fiction included, which is by author. Data: title,
author, periodical, volume, pages, date.

Subject Index to Periodicals. London: Library Association, 1919
to date. (Originally, *Athenaeum Subject Index*.)

Dates covered: 1915 to date in annual volumes. Field: British and American general periodicals. Some duplication of *Reader's Guide*. Arrangement:
alphabetical by subject; arranged by author in earlier volumes.

Ulrich's International Periodicals Directory. New York: R. R.
Bowker Company, 1965.

A world-wide listing of titles.

NEWSPAPERS

Directory of Newspapers and Periodicals (formerly *American
Newspaper Annual and Directory*). Philadelphia, Pa.: N. W.
Ayer and Son, 1880 to date.

New York Times Index.

Dates: 1913 to date. Issued semimonthly. Field: serves as an index to
other newspapers, which cover many of the same subjects at the same time

and, through their common news services, print many of the same articles.
Arrangement: alphabetical index; references by day, year, page, column.

Times, London. *Official Index*.
Dates: 1906 to date. Now issued quarterly.

PUBLIC DOCUMENTS

Catalogs.

Monthly Catalog of United States Public Documents. Washington, D.C.: U. S. Government Printing Office, 1895 to date.

U. S. Library of Congress. *Monthly Check-List of State Publications*. Washington, D. C.: U. S. Government Printing Office, 1910 to date.

Guides.

Boyd, Anne M. *United States Government Publications as Sources of Information for Libraries*. New York: H. W. Wilson Company, 3rd edition, revised, 1950.

Hirshberg, Herbert S. and Melinat, Carl H. *Subject Guide to United States Government Publications*. Chicago: American Library Association, 1947.

Leidy, W. P. *A Popular Guide to Government Publications*. New York: Columbia University Press, 3rd edition, 1968.

GUIDES FOR SELECTING BOOKS

What books or articles are best for a particular purpose? For what use is a given book best fitted? The following works help in answering such questions.

Guides to Reference Books and Indexes.

Minto, John. *Reference Books*. London: Library Association, 1929; Supplement, 1931.

Shores, Louis. *Basic Reference Sources*. Chicago: American Library Association, 1954.

Walford, A. J. *Guide to Reference Material*. 3 vols. New York: R. R. Bowker Company, 1966-1968.

Winchell, Constance M. *Guide to Reference Books*. Chicago: American Library Association, 8th edition, 1967.

A new edition of the standard work of Isadore G. Mudge. Classified and annotated, American compilation. The fullest, most useful work of its kind.

Guides to Books in General

A.L.A. Booklist. Chicago: American Library Association, 1905 to date.

> A convenient form of this material (in two volumes, with periodic supplements) is known as the *A.L.A. Catalog*. The list is compiled to guide librarians in purchasing, but it is useful to readers and students. Brief descriptive notes by experts indicate the use and value of the various books.

A.L.A. Index. Boston, Mass.: American Library Association, 1901. Supplement, 1914.

> Years covered: 1900-1910. Plan: a subject index of material in miscellaneous books generally found in libraries.

Book Review Digest. New York: H. W. Wilson Company, 1905 to date.

> Issued monthly, cumulated semiannually and annually.

Cook, Dorothy E. and West, Dorothy H. *Standard Catalog for Public Libraries.* New York: H. W. Wilson Company, 4th edition, 1958. Annual Supplements.

Guide to the Study of the United States of America: Representative Books Reflecting the Development of American Life and Thought. R. P. Basler and others, comps. Library of Congress, 1960.

Murphey, Robert W. *How and Where to Look It Up: A Guide to Standard Sources of Information*. New York: McGraw-Hill Book Company, 1958.

Hoffman, Hester. *The Reader's Adviser and Bookman's Manual.* New York: R. R. Bowker Company, 10th edition, 1964.

Paperbound Books in Print. New York: R. R. Bowker Company. 1955 to date. Monthly.

Sonnenschein, William S. *Best Books*. London: Routledge and Kegan Paul, Ltd.; New York: G. P. Putnam's Sons, 3rd edition, 1910-1935.

> About 100,000 books classified by various departments of knowledge.

Technical Book Review Index. Pittsburgh, Pa.: The Library, 1917-1929; New York: Special Libraries Association, 1935 to date.

> Quarterly index. Covers reviews in technical periodicals.

INCLUSIVE LISTS OF BOOKS

It is possible by these and similar lists to get bibliographical data about almost any book ever published in America. Data given: author's name, title, date, paging, size. All works in the following list, except the Evans, give the publisher's retail price. Similar lists cover books published in Canada, England, France, Germany, Belgium, Denmark, Italy, the Netherlands, Norway, Spain and Spanish America, Sweden, Switzerland. Most libraries keep such books in their order departments. For fuller details, see the *Guide to Reference Books.*

Catalogs of Books in Print.

1900-1928. *United States Catalog; Books in Print.* First edition, 1900; periodic supplements; fourth edition, 1928. New York: H. W. Wilson Company.

1928 to date. *Cumulative Book Index.* New York: H. W. Wilson Company.

Published monthly (except August) and cumulated. Includes books published in English anywhere in the world. Published since 1898, but earlier issues are superseded by the *United States Catalog.*

Catalogs of Older American Books.

The dates before entries indicate publishing years covered.

1639-1820. Evans, Charles. *American Bibliography.* Chicago: Privately Printed, 12 vols., 1903-1934.

Never completed. Includes all books, pamphlets, and periodical publications down to 1799, in the present volumes. Chronologically arranged, with indexes. Locates copies when possible.

1820-1861. Roorbach, O. A. *Bibliotheca Americana,* 1820-1861. New York: O. A. Roorbach, 1852-1861.

Arranged alphabetically by author and title.

1861-1871. Kelly, James. *American Catalogue of Books Published in the United States from January, 1861, to January, 1871.* New York: John Wiley and Sons, 1866-1871. Reprinted by Peter Smith, New York, 1938.

1876-1910. *American Catalogue of Books, 1876-1910.* New York: R. R. Bowker Company, 1880-1911. Reprinted by Peter Smith, 1941.

Arrangement by author, title, and subject.

YEARBOOKS AND ALMANACS

Annuals and yearbooks cover almost as wide a field as encyclopedias, to which they may serve as supplements. The annual almanacs, published more hurriedly, are often less accurate than the best yearbooks. The date on an almanac is the date of publication; the almanac covers the preceding year. The date on a yearbook is that of the year covered in the book. Only the latest volume of an almanac may be needed, for earlier material still useful is generally reprinted in each issue. But the older volumes of a yearbook are more likely to be permanently useful.

American Year Book. New York: Publisher varies, 1910 to date.
> Table of contents and index in each volume. International scope, American point of view. Authors' names given for most articles.

Americana Annual. New York and Chicago: Americana Corporation, 1923 to date.
> Annual supplement to *Encyclopedia Americana.* Date like an almanac, to cover the preceding year. Illustrated.

Annual Register. London: Longmans, Green and Company, 1761 to date.
> Annual review of history, literature, science, art, drama, music, finance, and commerce. Emphasis upon England. Obituaries of eminent persons who died during the year. Subject index.

Book of the States. Chicago: Council of State Governments, 1935 to date. Biennial.

Britannica Book of the Year. Chicago: Encyclopaedia Britannica, Inc., 1937 to date.
> Annual supplement to the *Encyclopaedia Britannica.* Illustrated.

Information Please Almanac. New York: The Macmillan Company, 1947 to date.
> Annual which presents up-to-date statistical and miscellaneous facts about a variety of subjects.

New International Year Book. New York: Dodd, Mead and Company, 1908-1931. Funk and Wagnalls, 1932 to date.
> Began as an annual supplement to the *New International Encyclopedia* (now out of print), which it resembles in arrangement. Illustrated.

Statesman's Yearbook. London: The Macmillan Company, 1864 to date.
> Covers governments, industries, and resources of the various countries. Bibliography of official publications for each country. Index.

Statistical Abstracts of the United States. Washington, D. C.: U. S. Government Printing Office, 1878 to date.

> Government statistics on population, trade, employment, and numerous other subjects.

Whitaker, Joseph. *Almanack.* London: Joseph Whitaker and Sons, 1869 to date.

> Government statistics, especially of the British Empire. Index after Table of Contents.

World Almanac. New York: Newspaper Enterprise Association, Inc. (formerly *New York World-Telegram and The Sun*), 1868 to date.

> Widely diversified content chiefly American, fullest for New York City. Index at the front.

Yearbook of the United Nations. New York: Columbia University Press, 1946 to date.

> A review of United Nations activities.

GAZETTEERS AND ATLASES

A common index for the whole volume enables one to find places on the various maps. Much useful information supplements the maps. A historical atlas may be necessary for some kinds of research, but for other kinds recently revised maps are more likely to be needed.

Columbia Lippincott Gazetteer of the World. New York: Columbia University Press, 1962.

Muir's Atlas of Ancient and Classical History. Reprinted by Barnes and Noble, Inc., New York, 2nd edition, 1961.

Muir's Historical Atlas: Ancient, Medieval and Modern. Edited by Harold Fullard and R. F. Treharne. Reprinted by Barnes and Noble, Inc., New York, 9th edition, 1962.

Muir's Historical Atlas: Medieval and Modern. Edited by George Goodall and R. F. Treharne. New York: Barnes and Noble, Inc., 9th edition, 1962.

Rand McNally's New Cosmopolitan World Atlas. Chicago: Rand McNally & Co., 1967.

Shepherd, William Robert. *Historical Atlas.* New York: Barnes and Noble, Inc., 9th edition, 1964.

SECOND DIVISION
Special Fields

PHILOSOPHY, PSYCHOLOGY (Library Number 100)
Philosophy.

Avey, Albert E. *Handbook in the History of Philosophy.* New York: Barnes and Noble, Inc., 2nd edition, 1961.

Baldwin, James Mark. *Dictionary of Philosophy and Psychology.* New York: The Macmillan Company, 1901-1905. Reprinted by Peter Smith, Gloucester, Mass., 1949.

Psychology.

Daniel, Robert S. and Louttit, Chauncey M. *Professional Problems in Psychology.* New York: Prentice-Hall, Inc., 1953.

Harvard University. *List of Books on Psychology.* Cambridge, Mass.: Harvard University Press, 3rd edition, 1964.

Psychological Abstracts. Washington, D. C.: American Psychological Association, 1927 to date.
Monthly bibliography, with signed abstracts.

Psychological Index. Princeton, N. J.: Psychological Review Company, 1894-1935.
Annual bibliography, with signed abstracts.

Warren, Howard C. *Dictionary of Psychology.* Boston, Mass.: Houghton Mifflin Company, 1934.

RELIGION (Library Number 200)

Hastings, James. *Dictionary of the Bible.* New York: Charles Scribner's Sons, revised edition, 1963.
For further references on the Bible, see Literature, Concordances.

The Interpreter's Bible. 12 vols. Nashville, Tenn.: Abingdon-Cokesbury Press, 1951-1957.
The King James and Revised Standard Versions, with commentaries.

Mead, Frank S. *Handbook of Denominations in the United States.* Nashville, Tenn.: Abingdon-Cokesbury Press, 4th edition, 1965.

SOCIOLOGY (Library Number 300)

Encyclopedia of the Social Sciences. New York: The Macmillan Company, 1930-1935. 15 vols. Reissued in 8 vols., 1948.

London Bibliography of the Social Sciences. London: London School of Economics, 1931 to date.

Public Affairs Information Service Bulletin. New York: Public Affairs Information Service, 1915 to date.

Weekly with bi-monthly and annual cumulations. Field: political science, economics, sociology, commerce, finance.

World List of Social Science Periodicals (UNESCO). New York: International Documents Service—Columbia University Press, 2nd edition, 1957.

Business.

Allen, Roy G. D. and Ely, J. Edward. *International Trade Statistics.* New York: John Wiley and Sons, Inc., 1953.

Coman, E. T. *Sources of Business Information.* Berkeley: University of California Press, 2nd edition, 1964.

Manley, Marian C. *Business Information: How to Find and Use It.* New York: Harper and Brothers, 1955.

Munn, Glenn G. *Encyclopedia of Banking and Finance.* New York: Bankers Publishing Company, 6th edition, 1962.

Sloan, H. S. and Zurcher, A. J. *Dictionary of Economics.* New York: Barnes and Noble, Inc., 4th edition, 1961.

Education.

Alexander, Carter and Burke, Arvid J. *How to Locate Educational Information and Data.* New York: Columbia University Teachers College, 4th edition, revised and enlarged, 1958.

Education Index. New York: H. W. Wilson Company, 1932 to date.

Covers 1929 to date. Indexes 150 periodicals and much other material. Kept up to date by monthly issues cumulated into annual volumes.

Harris, Chester, ed. *Encyclopedia of Educational Research.* New York: The Macmillan Company, 3rd edition, 1960.

Monroe, Paul. *Cyclopedia of Education.* 5 vols. New York. The Macmillan Company, 1911-1913.

United Nations Educational, Scientific, and Cultural Organization. Education Clearing House. *Education Abstracts.* Paris: 1949 to date. Monthly.

United States Bureau of Education. *Educational Directory.* Washington, D. C.: U. S. Government Printing Office, 1912 to date.

As a chapter in the annual report of the Commissioner of Education, this work goes back to 1895. Lists educational officials in the United States.

United States Office of Education. Library. *Bibliography of Research Studies in Education,* 1926, 1927-1939, 1940. Washington, D. C.: U. S. Government Printing Office, 1929-1942.

Available as bulletins of the Bureau of Education, 1928-1940. An annual list of studies in education. Discontinued during World War II.

Government.

Cyclopedia of American Government. 3 vols. New York: D. Appleton and Company, 1914. Reprinted by Peter Smith, 1949.

Includes many general and foreign subjects.

Documents on American Foreign Relations. Published for the Council on Foreign Relations. New York: Harper and Brothers, 1952 to date. Annual.

Public Administration Organizations. Chicago: Public Administration Clearing House, 1932 to date. Biennial.

Seckler-Hudson, Catheryn. *Bibliography on Public Administration.* Washington, D.C.: American University Press, 4th edition, 1953.

Smith, Edward C. and Zurcher, Arnold J. *Dictionary of American Politics.* New York: Barnes and Noble, Inc., 2nd edition, 1968.

United States Government Organization Manual. Washington, D. C.: U. S. Government Printing Office, 1935 to date.

Law.

Ballentine, James Arthur. *Law Dictionary with Pronunciations.* Rochester, N. Y.: Lawyers Co-operative Publishing Company, revised edition, 1948.

United States Code . . . Containing the General and Permanent Laws of the United States in Force on January 2, 1947. 5 vols. Washington, D. C.: U. S. Government Printing Office, 1947-1948. Supplements, 1948 to date.

PHILOLOGY (Library Number 400)

Bibliography.

Besterman, Theodore. *World Bibliography of Bibliographies.* 4 vols. Geneva: Societas Bibliographica, 3rd edition, 1955.

Cross, T. P. *Bibliographical Guide to English Studies.* Chicago: University of Chicago Press, 10th edition, 1951.

Kennedy, Arthur G. *A Concise Bibliography for Students of English,* Stanford, Calif.: Stanford University Press, revised edition, 1960.

Dictionaries.

Besides spelling, pronunciation, derivation, and definition of words, modern dictionaries contain a great variety of information. Perhaps only by habitual use can one learn to take full advantage of the resources in historical and scientific tables, dates, and illustrations.

American College Dictionary. New York: Random House, 1964.

Britannica World Language Dictionary. 2 vols. New York: Funk and Wagnalls Company, 1954.

Part I is the complete *New Practical Standard Dictionary* of the English language. Part II includes common words in six languages: French, German, Italian, Spanish, Swedish, and Yiddish.

Craigie, William A. and Hulbert, James R. *Dictionary of American English on Historical Principles.* 4 vols. Chicago: University of Chicago Press, 1938-1944.

Historical treatment with quotations from authors.

Funk and Wagnalls' New Standard Dictionary of the English Language. New York: Funk and Wagnalls Company, 1913. Revised edition, 1952.

Excellent for present-day meanings; less good for obsolete words. Proper names included in the general alphabetical list. The only general dictionary to give antonyms as well as synonyms. Useful abridgement: *Desk Standard Dictionary.*

New Century Dictionary. 2 vols. New York: Appleton-Century-Crofts, new edition, 1956.

Though based on the old *Century Dictionary and Cyclopedia,* this edition has been entirely rewritten, with much new material added.

New English Dictionary on Historical Principles. 10 vols. Oxford: Clarendon Press, 1888-1933. Reprinted as the *Oxford English Dictionary,* in 12 vols. and a supplementary volume, 1933.

Sometimes referred to as *Murray's Dictionary,* the *Oxford Dictionary,* or *N.E.D. (New English Dictionary).* The most scholarly English dictionary. For each word it attempts a full history since 1150. Invaluable when full information is needed. Useful abridgements: *Concise Oxford Dictionary of Current English,* 4th edition, 1951; *Universal Oxford Dictionary on Historical Principles,* revised edition, 1955; and *American Oxford Dictionary,* enlarged edition, 1935, which prefers correct American usage when it differs from that of England.

Webster's New International Dictionary of the English Language.
Springfield, Mass.: G. & C. Merriam Company, 2nd edition,
1954. (3rd edition, 1961, emphasizes current usage.)
    Largest vocabulary in any general dictionary. Useful abridgement:
    Webster's Collegiate Dictionary.

Webster's New World Dictionary of the American Language. 2
vols. Cleveland, Ohio: World Publishing Company, 1951.

Wyld, H. C. K. *Universal Dictionary of the English Language.*
New York: E. P. Dutton and Company, 1932.

Synonym Dictionaries.

The exact meaning of a word is often best understood by
comparing the word with synonyms, that is, with other words of
similar but slightly different meanings. General dictionaries differ-
entiate synonyms, but special and often more detailed treatment
may be found in the following works.

Allen, F. Sturges. *Allen's Synonyms and Antonyms.* New York:
Harper and Brothers, revised edition, 1949.
    List alphabetical. Words characterized as "rare," "bookish," etc. No dis-
    cussion or comparison of meanings. A good modern list.

Crabb, George. *English Synonyms.* New York: Grosset and
Dunlap, revised edition, 1945.
    Antonyms not given. Words of similar meanings given in groups, with
    differences of meanings discriminated. Cross references, but no index.

Fernald, James C. *Standard Handbook of Synonyms, Antonyms
and Prepositions.* New York: Funk and Wagnalls Company,
revised edition, 1947.
    Arrangement as in Crabb; more extensive, with synonyms and antonyms.

March, Francis A. and March, Francis A., Jr. *Thesaurus Dictionary.* Garden City, New York: Hanover House, 1958.
    Long alphabetical lists of words for general ideas, with synonyms and
    antonyms in parallel columns. Cross references, but no index.

Roget, Peter M. *Thesaurus of English Words and Phrases.* London: Longmans, Green and Company, revised edition, 1962;
New York: St. Martin's Press, revised edition, 1962.
    See also Mawson's *International Thesaurus of English Words and
    Phrases* (revised, 1946), which embodies Roget's original book.

Webster's Dictionary of Synonyms. Springfield, Mass.: G. & C.
Merriam Company, 1951.

Usage.

Curme, George O. *English Grammar*. New York: Barnes and Noble, Inc., 1947.

Dictionary of Americanisms on Historical Principles. 2 vols. Edited by Mitford M. Mathews. Chicago: University of Chicago Press, 1951. Unabridged 1 vol. edition, 1956.

Evans, Bergen and Cornelia. *Dictionary of Contemporary American Usage*. New York: Random House, 1957.

Fowler, Henry Watson. *Dictionary of Modern English Usage*. New York: Oxford University Press, 2nd edition, 1965.

Nicholson, Margaret. *Dictionary of American-English Usage*. New York: Oxford University Press, 1957.

Wyld, Henry C. *A History of Modern Colloquial English*. New York: Barnes and Noble, Inc. 3rd edition, revised, reprinted 1963.

SCIENCE (Library Number 500)

Harper Encyclopedia of Science. 4 vols. Edited by James R. Newman. New York: Harper and Row, 1963.

Hawkins, Reginald R. *Scientific, Medical, and Technical Books Published in the United States of America*. New York: R. R. Bowker Company, 2nd edition, 1958.

Van Nostrand's Scientific Encyclopedia. New York: D. Van Nostrand Company, 3rd edition, 1958.

Biology.

Biological Abstracts. Philadelphia, Pa.: University of Pennsylvania, 1926 to date.
Continues the older *Abstracts of Bacteriology* and *Botanical Abstracts*.

Botany.

American Joint Committee on Horticultural Nomenclature. *Standardized Plant Names*. Harrisburg, Pa.: J. Horace McFarland Company, 2nd edition, 1942.

Willis, J. C. *Dictionary of the Flowering Plants and Ferns*. London: Cambridge University Press, 7th edition, 1967.

Chemistry and Pharmacy.

British Chemical Abstracts. London: Bureau of Chemical Abstracts, 1926-1953.

Chemical Abstracts. Easton, Pa.: American Chemical Society, 1907 to date.

Condensed Chemical Dictionary. New York: Reinhold Publishing Corporation, 6th edition, revised and enlarged, 1961.

Mellon, M. G. *Chemical Publications.* New York: McGraw-Hill Book Company, 4th edition, 1965.

Pharmacopoeia of the United States of America. Easton, Pa.: Mack Publishing Company, 15th revised edition, 1955.

Thorpe, Jocelyn F. and Whitley, M. A. *Dictionary of Applied Chemistry.* 12 vols. and Index. New York: Longmans, Green and Company, 4th edition, revised and enlarged, 1937-1955.

Geography and Geology.

Annotated Bibliography of Economic Geology. Urbana, Ill.: Economic Geology Publishing Company, 1929 to date.
   Published annually.

Bibliography of North American Geology, 1948. Washington, D. C.: U. S. Government Printing Office, 1950.

International Geological Congress ... 1933 ... *Guide Book.* Washington, D. C.: U. S. Government Printing Office, 1932-1933.
   For the United States. Illustrations, plates, maps, tables.

Nickles, John M. and Miller, Robert B. *Bibliography and Index of Geology Exclusive of North America.* Washington, D. C.: Geological Society of America, 1934 to date. Biennial.

Pearl, Richard M. *Guide to Geologic Literature.* New York: McGraw-Hill Book Company, 1951.

Webster's Geographical Dictionary. Springfield, Mass.: G. & C. Merriam Company, revised edition, 1966.

Wright, John K. and Platt, Elizabeth T. *Aids to Geographical Research.* New York: Columbia University Press, 2nd edition, revised, 1947.
   A list of bibliographies, periodicals, and reference works.

Ethnology.

Locke, Alain and Stern, Bernhard J. *When Peoples Meet.* New York: Barnes and Noble, Inc., revised edition, 1946.
   Summaries of race and culture by 85 scholars.

Peoples of all Nations. London: Fleetway House, 1922-1924.
Photographs, color plates, maps.

Mathematics and Physics.

James, Glenn and James, Robert C. *Mathematics Dictionary.* New York: D. Van Nostrand Company, 3rd edition, 1968.

Parke, Nathan G. *Guide to the Literature of Mathematics and Physics.* New York: Dover Publications, 2nd edition, 1959.

Science Abstracts . . . Section A, Physics. London: 1898 to date. Monthly. Publisher varies.

United Nations Atomic Energy Commission Group. *An International Bibliography on Atomic Energy.* 2 vols. and Supplements. New York: Columbia University Press, 1949 to date.

World of Mathematics. Edited by James R. Newman. New York: Simon & Schuster, Inc., 4 vols., 1956.

Meteorology and Mineralogy.

Berry, F. A., Jr., Bollay, E., and Beers, N. R *Handbook of Meteorology.* New York: McGraw-Hill Book Company, 1945.

A Glossary of the Mining and Mineral Industry. Washington, D. C.: U. S. Government Printing Office, 1920. Reprinted 1947.

Mineralogical Abstracts. London: Simpkin, Marshall, Ltd., 1922 to date.

Minerals Yearbook. Washington, D. C.: U. S. Government Printing Office, 1933 to date.

Pearl, Richard M. *Rocks and Minerals.* New York: Barnes and Noble, Inc., 1956.

Royal Meteorological Society, London. *Bibliography of Meteorological Literature.* London: Royal Meteorological Society, 1922 to date.

Thiessen, Alfred H. *Weather Glossary.* Washington, D. C.: U. S. Government Printing Office, 1946.

Natural History.

Altsheler, Brent. *Natural History Index-Guide.* New York: H. W. Wilson Company, 2nd edition, 1940.

Cambridge Natural History. 10 vols. London and New York: The Macmillan Company, 1891-1905.
Gives bibliographic references.

Zoology.

Audubon, John James. *Birds of America.* New York: The Macmillan Company, new edition, edited by William Vogt, 1953.

Bartholomew, J. G. *Atlas of Zoögeography.* Edinburgh: John Bartholomew and Son, Ltd., 1911.
  Maps, bibliography. Includes mammals, birds, reptiles, amphibians, fishes, molluscs, insects.

Dean, Bashford. *Bibliography of Fishes.* 3 vols. New York: Russell and Russell, Inc., 1962.

Hall, Thomas S. *Source Book in the History of Animal Biology.* New York: McGraw-Hill Book Company, 1951.

Smith, Roger C., and Painter, R. H. *Guide to the Literature of the Zoological Sciences.* Minneapolis: Burgess Publishing Company, 7th edition, 1967.

Zoological Record. London: Zoological Society of London, 1862 to date.

USEFUL ARTS (Library Number 600)

Aeronautics and Astronautics

Jane's All the World's Aircraft. Edited by Leonard Bridgman. New York: McGraw-Hill Book Company, 1909 to date.
  Comprehensive data; photographs. Revised annually.

Progress in Astronautics and Aeronautics. Edited by Martin Summerfield. 20 vols. New York: Academic Press.

World Aviation Annual. New York: Aviation Research Institute, 1948 to date.

Agriculture.

Agricultural Index. New York: H. W. Wilson Company, 1916 to date.
  System: cumulative. Field: agricultural periodicals, state, federal, and foreign agricultural publications. Arrangement: alphabetical by subject.

Bailey, Liberty H. and Bailey, Ethel Z. *Hortus: a Concise Dictionary of Gardening, General Horticulture and Cultivated Plants in North America.* New York: The Macmillan Company, 1930. Revised edition, entitled *Hortus Second,* 1941.

Bailey, Liberty H. *Standard Cyclopedia of Horticulture.* New York: The Macmillan Company, 1914-1917; 6 vols. Reissued in 3 vols., 1947.

U. S. Department of Agriculture. *Bibliography of Agriculture.* Washington, D. C.: U. S. Government Printing Office, 1942 to date.

Monthly listing of pamphlets, articles, and books.

U. S. Office of Experiment Stations. *Experiment Station Record.* Washington, D. C.: U. S. Government Printing Office, 1890 to 1948.

Abstracts serving practically as an index of agricultural literature in English and principal foreign languages.

Yearbook of Food and Agricultural Statistics. Rome: United Nations Food and Agricultural Organization, 1948 to date.

Army and Navy.

Army Almanac. Washington, D. C.: U. S. Government Printing Office, 1950.

Brassy's Naval Shipping Annual. London: William Clowes and Sons, 1886 to date.

Title and publishers have changed at times.

Laws Relating to Veterans. 2 vols.: 1914-1941, 1941-1951. Washington, D. C.: U. S. Government Printing Office, 1950-1951. Supplement, 1956.

Official Army Register. Washington, D. C.: U. S. Government Printing Office. Annual.

United States Navy Regulations. Washington, D. C.: U. S. Government Printing Office, 1948. Periodic supplements.

Engineering.

For works in the special kinds of engineering (Chemical, Civil, Electrical, Mechanical, Railroad, Structural) see Winchell, *Guide to Reference Works.*

Dalton, Blanche H. *Sources of Engineering Information.* Berkeley, Calif.: University of California Press, 1949.

Engineer's Year-Book. London: Morgan Brothers, Ltd., 1894 to date.

Engineering Index (title varies). New York: Engineering Magazine, 1892-1919; American Society of Mechanical Engineers, 1920-1934. Engineering Index, Inc., 1934 to date.

1884-1905 in 4 vols. Annual vols., 1906 to date. Field: foreign and American technical journals and other publications.

Engineering Materials Manual. Edited by T. C. Du Mond. New York: Reinhold Publishing Corporation, 1951.

Jones, Franklin Day. *Engineering Encyclopedia*. New York: Industrial Press, 3rd edition, 1963.

Lombardo, Josef and others. *Engineering Drawing*. New York: Barnes and Noble, Inc., revised edition, 1956.
   Contains American Standards Association drawings and tables.

Home Economics.

Iowa State College of Agriculture and Mechanic Arts. *Basic Books and Periodicals in Home Economics*. Ames, Iowa: Iowa State College, 1942. Supplement 1941-1947, 1949.

Winton, Andrew L., and Winton, Kate B. *Structure and Composition of Foods*. 4 vols. New York: John Wiley and Sons, Inc., 1932-1939.

Industrial Arts.

Industrial Arts Index. New York: H. W. Wilson Company, 1913 to date.
   Field: engineering, business, trade periodicals, some pamphlets and government publications. Some foreign periodicals.

New York Public Library. *New Technical Books*. New York: Library, 1915 to date. Bimonthly.

Journalism.

Ayer, N. W. and Son. *Directory of Newspapers and Periodicals*. Philadelphia, Pa.: N. W. Ayer and Son, 1880 to date.

Ford, E. H. *A Bibliography of Literary Journalism in America*. Minneapolis, Minn.: Burgess Publishing Company, 1937.

Mott, George Fox and others. *New Survey of Journalism*. New York: Barnes and Noble, Inc., 4th edition, revised, 1958.

Wolseley, R. E. *The Journalist's Bookshelf*. Philadelphia, Pa.: Chilton Books, 7th edition, 1961.

Medicine.

Cornell Conferences on Therapy. 7 vols. New York: The Macmillan Company, 1946-1955.

Current List of Medical Literature. Washington, D. C.: Army Medical Library, 1941 to date.

Dorland, William A. N. *Dorland's Illustrated Medical Dictionary*. Philadelphia, Pa., and London: W. B. Saunders Company, 24th edition, 1965.

Index Medicus. New York, Boston, Mass., and Washington, D. C.: 1879-1926.

Quarterly Cumulative Index Medicus. Chicago: American Medical Association, 1927 to date.

Textbook of Medicine. Edited by Russell L. Cecil and Robert F. Loeb. Philadelphia, Pa.: W. B. Saunders Company, 10th edition, 1959.

Mining and Metallurgy.

U. S. Bureau of Mines and U. S. Geological Survey. *Mineral Resources of the United States*. Washington, D. C.: Public Affairs Press, 1948.

Printing and Publishing.

Collins, Frederick H. *Authors' and Printers' Dictionary*. London: Oxford University Press, 10th edition, revised, 1956.

Melcher, Daniel, and Larrick, Nancy. *Printing and Promotion Handbook*. New York: McGraw-Hill Book Company, 3rd edition, 1966.

The Literary Market Place. New York: R. R. Bowker Company. Annual directory of American book publishing.

Radio and Television.

American Radio Relay League. *Radio Amateur's Handbook*. West Hartford, Conn.: American Radio Relay League. Annual.

Manly, Harold P. *Radio-Television-Electronic Dictionary*. Chicago: Frederick J. Drake and Company, 1960.

Telecommunication Convention Final Protocol and Radio Regulations. Washington, D. C.: U. S. Government Printing Office, 1950.

Television Manual. New York: J. F. Rider, Inc., 1948 to date.

FINE ARTS (Library Number 700)

Indexes and General Works.

Art Index. New York: H. W. Wilson Company, 1933 to date.

American Art Directory.   New York: R. R. Bowker Company, 1899 to date.

Christensen, Erwin O. *The Index of American Design.* New York: The Macmillan Company, 1950.

Gardner, Helen. *Art through the Ages.* New York: Harcourt, Brace and Company, 4th edition, 1959.

Reinach, Salomon. *Apollo; an illustrated Manual of the History of Art.* New York: Charles Scribner's Sons, 1935.

Vincent, Jean Anne. *History of Art.* New York: Barnes and Noble, Inc., 1955.

Architecture.

Fletcher, Sir Banister F. *History of Architecture.* New York: Charles Scribner's Sons, 17th edition, 1961.

Hamlin, Talbot. *Forms and Functions of Twentieth-Century Architecture.* New York: Columbia University Press, 1952. 4 vols.

Ceramics.

American Ceramic Society. *Ceramic Abstracts.* Easton, Pa.: American Ceramics Society, 1922 to date. Annual volumes.

Searle, Alfred B. *Encyclopedia of the Ceramic Industries.* London: Ernest Benn, Ltd., 1930.

Dancing.

Chujoy, Anatole. *Dance Encyclopedia.* New York: A. S. Barnes and Company, 1949.

Engraving.

Zigrosser, Carl. *The Book of Fine Prints.* New York: Crown Publishers, Inc., revised edition, 1956.

Music.

Apel, Willi. *Harvard Dictionary of Music.* Cambridge, Mass.: Harvard University Press, 1944.

Grove, Sir George. *Grove's Dictionary of Music and Musicians.* 9 vols. New York: St. Martin's Press, 5th edition, 1954. Supplement, 1961.

Kobbe, Gustav. *Complete Opera Book.* New York: G. P. Putnam's Sons, new edition, revised by the Earl of Harewood, 1963.

Oxford Companion to Music. London: Oxford University Press, 9th edition, revised, 1955.

Peltz, Mary Ellis, ed. *Introduction to Opera.* New York: Barnes and Noble, Inc., 2nd edition, 1962.

Thompson, Oscar. *International Cyclopedia of Music and Musicians.* New York: Dodd, Mead and Company, 9th edition, 1964.

The Music Index. Detroit, Mich.: Information Service, Inc., 1949 to date.

Painting.

Myers, Bernard S., ed. *Encyclopedia of Painting.* New York: Crown Publishers, Inc., 1955.

Robb, David. *The Harper History of Painting.* New York: Harper and Brothers, 1951.

Photography.

American Annual of Photography. Boston, Mass.: American Photographic Publishing Company, 1887 to date.

Monthly Abstract Bulletin from the Kodak Research Laboratories. Rochester, N. Y.: Eastman Kodak Company, 1915 to date.

LITERATURE (Library Number 800)

Bibliography.

Annual Bibliography of English Language and Literature. New York: Cambridge University Press, 1921 to date.

For English and American literature. Good for both English and American scholarship.

Bibliographical Society of America. *Bibliography of American Literature.* Compiled by Jacob Blanck. 3 vols. New Haven: Yale University Press, 1955-1959.

Publications of the Modern Language Association of America.

An annual list is published in each volume. For modern languages.

Year's Work in English Studies. New York: Oxford University Press, 1921 to date.

For English literature.

Year's Work in Modern Language Studies. New York: Cambridge University Press, 1929 to date.

For modern languages. Does not cover English.

Literary Histories and Handbooks.

The best works on foreign literatures are written in the languages concerned. A few translations and original English works are here recommended.

Baugh, Albert C. and Others. *A Literary History of England.* New York: Appleton-Century-Crofts, Inc., 1948.

Benét, William R. *The Reader's Encyclopedia.* New York: T. Y. Crowell Company, 2nd edition, 1965.

Brewer, Ebenezer C. *Dictionary of Phrase and Fable.* New York: Harper and Row, 8th revised edition, 1964.

Cambridge History of American Literature. New York: G. P. Putnam's Sons, 1917-1921. Reprinted, 1943.

Cambridge History of English Literature. 15 vols. London: Cambridge University Press, 1907-1927. Reprinted without bibliographies, 1933. Home Study edition, 1950.

Columbia Dictionary of Modern European Literature. Edited by Horatio Smith. New York: Columbia University Press, 1947.

Crawford, B. V. and Others. *American Literature.* New York: Barnes and Noble, Inc., 3rd edition, 1953.

Esdaile, Arundell. *A Student's Manual of Bibliography.* Revised by Roy Stokes. New York: Barnes and Noble, Inc., 3rd revised edition, 1955.

Friederich, Werner P. *Outline-History of German Literature.* New York: Barnes and Noble, Inc., 2nd edition, 1961.

Gardner, Edmund G. *Italy; a Companion to Italian Studies.* London: Methuen and Company, Ltd., 1934.

Hart, James D. *Oxford Companion to American Literature.* New York: Oxford University Press, 4th edition, 1965.

Harvey, Paul. *Oxford Companion to Classical Literature.* New York: Oxford University Press, 2nd edition, 1937.

Harvey, Paul. *Oxford Companion to English Literature.* New York: Oxford University Press, 4th edition, 1967.

Harvey, Paul and Heseltine, J. E. *Oxford Companion to French Literature.* New York: Oxford University Press, 1959.

New Century Handbook of English Literature. Edited by Clarence L. Barnhart. New York: Appleton-Century-Crofts, Inc., 1956.

Otis, W. B. and Needleman, M. H. *Outline-History of English Literature.* 2 vols. New York: Barnes and Noble, Inc., 4th edition of Vol. I, revised 1960, 2nd edition of Vol. II, revised 1957.

Oxford History of English Literature. New York: Oxford University Press, 1945-. (In progress; to be 12 vols.)

Rose, Herbert J. *Handbook of Greek Literature.* New York: E. P. Dutton and Company, revised edition, 1948.

Slonim, Marc. *Outline of Russian Literature.* New York: Oxford University Press, 1958.

Spiller, Robert E., *et al. Literary History of the United States.* New York: The Macmillan Company, 3rd edition, 1963. Bibliography supplement, 1964.

Teuffel, W. S. *History of Roman Literature.* London: H. W. Bell, 1900. Translated from the German by C. W. Warr.

Trawick, Buckner B. *World Literature.* 2 vols. New York: Barnes and Noble, Inc., 1953-1955.

Wells, John E. *Manual of the Writings in Middle English, 1050-1400.* New Haven, Conn.: Yale University Press, 1914-1941. 9 Supplements, 1941-1952.

Zesmer, David M. *Guide to English Literature from Beowulf through Chaucer and Medieval Drama.* New York: Barnes and Noble, Inc., 1961.

Allusions, Proverbs, Quotations.

Collections of quotations may enable one to find: (1) a quotation appropriate to a given subject or occasion, (2) the source and exact form of a quotation, or (3) passages most often quoted.

Bartlett, John. *Familiar Quotations.* Boston, Mass.: Little, Brown and Company, 13th edition, 1955.

Passages, phrases, and proverbs from earliest times. Arrangement: chronological by authors; index of authors; index of important words.

Taylor, Archer. *Dictionary of American Proverbs and Proverbial Phrases, 1820–1880.* Cambridge, Mass.: Harvard University Press, 1959.

Champion, Selwyn. *Racial Proverbs.* New York: Barnes and Noble, Inc., 2nd edition, 1950.

Hoyt, Jehiel K. *Hoyt's New Cyclopedia of Practical Quotations.* New York: Funk and Wagnalls Company, revised edition, 1922. Revised by Kate Louise Roberts. Reissued 1940.

Arrangement: alphabetical by subjects; fully indexed; concordance of quotations from 3,000 authors.

Mencken, Henry L. *New Dictionary of Quotations on Historical Principles* . . . New York: Alfred A. Knopf, Inc., 1942.

Smith, William G. *Oxford Dictionary of English Proverbs*. New York: Oxford University Press, 2nd edition, 1948.

Stevenson, Burton E. *Home Book of Quotations*. New York: Dodd, Mead and Company, 9th revised edition, 1964.

The following works, similar in plan, are useful since their combined resources increase one's chances of finding a particular quotation.

Allibone, *Poetical Quotations from Chaucer to Tennyson; Prose Quotations from Socrates to Macaulay;* Benham, *Benham's Book of Quotations, Proverbs and Household Words;* Bent, *Familiar Short Sayings of Great Men;* Christy, *Proverbs, Maxims, and Phrases of All Ages;* Day, *Day's Collacon, an Encyclopaedia of Prose Quotations;* Hazlitt, *English Proverbs and Proverbial Phrases;* Prochnow, *Speaker's Handbook of Epigrams and Witticisms;* Walsh, *International Cyclopedia of Prose and Poetical Quotations from the Literature of the World.*

Criticism.

Allibone, Samuel A. *Critical Dictionary of English Literature and British and American Authors.* Philadelphia, Pa.: J. B. Lippincott Company, 1854-1871. Supplement, 1891.

Daiches, David. *A Critical History of English Literature.* 2 vols. New York: Ronald Press Company, 1960.

Moulton, Charles W. *Library of Literary Criticism of English and American Authors.* Buffalo, N. Y.: Charles W. Moulton, 1901-1905. Reprinted by Peter Smith, Gloucester, Mass., 1935-1940.

Wellek, René. *History of Modern Criticism.* New Haven: Yale University Press, 1955. 4 vols.

Concordances.

A concordance of any work lists the principal words of that work in alphabetical order, with exact references to the passages in which each word occurs. Thus the exact source and form of a quotation may be found, and revealing statistics may be gathered regarding the use of words.

Nelson's Complete Concordance of the Revised Standard Version of the Bible. New York: Thomas Nelson & Sons, 1957.

Strong, James. *Exhaustive Concordance to the Bible*. Nashville, Tenn.: Abingdon-Cokesbury. Reprinted periodically. (King James English version.)

Concordances are available for the following works and writers. For further bibliographical data about them, see the American Library Association's *Guide to Reference Books*. The names of compilers are here given in parentheses.

Aristophanes (Dunbar); Bede (Jones); *Beowulf* (Cook); Boethius (Cooper); Browning (Broughton and Stelter); Burns (Reid); Catallus (Wetmore); Chaucer (Tatlock and Kennedy); Coleridge (Logan); Collins (Booth and Jones); Cowper (Neve); Dante (Rand); Emerson (Hubbell.); Gray (Cook); Herbert (Mann); Herrick (MacLeod); Homer: *Iliad* (Prendergast), *Odyssey* and *Hymns* (Dunbar); Horace (Cooper); Keats (Baldwin); Kyd (Crawford); Marlowe (Crawford); Milton (Bradshaw); Omar Khayyam's *Rubaiyat* in the Fitzgerald translation (Tutin); Petrarch (McKenzie); Poe (Booth and Jones); Pope (Abbott); Shakespeare (Bartlett); Shelley (Ellis); Spenser (Osgood); Tennyson (Baker); Thomas á Kempis's *De Imitatione Christi* (Storr); Vergil (Wetmore); Wordsworth (Cooper).

Drama.

Dramatic Index. Boston, Mass.: Boston Book Company, 1910-1952.

Annual volumes. Material on drama and stage, from periodicals; also published plays.

The Players Library. London: Faber and Faber, Ltd., 1950.

Catalog of the Library of the British Drama League. Biennial supplements.

Firkins, Ina T. E. *Index to Plays, 1800-1926*. New York: H. W. Wilson Company, 1927. Supplement, 1927-1934, published, 1935.

Contents: English and American plays and English translations of foreign plays.

Nelms, Henning. *Play Production*. New York: Barnes and Noble, Inc., revised edition, 1958.

West, Dorothy H. and Peake, Dorothy M. *Play Index*. Vol. 1, *1949-1952*. Vol. 2, *1953-1960*. New York: H. W. Wilson Company, 1953, 1963.

Essays, Etc.

Essay and General Literature Index. New York. H. W. Wilson Company, 1934 to date.

Dates covered: 1900 to date. Semi-annual supplements cumulated annually. Contents: essays and articles in volumes of collections of essays or in miscellaneous works. Uses: (1) to find what essays an author has published; (2) to find who wrote a certain essay; (3) to find essays on a given topic; (4) to find information about a person; (5) to bring together criticisms of a given book or author; (6) to find different books, magazines, and collections which contain a given essay.

Fiction.

Baker, Ernest A. *The History of the English Novel.* 10 vols. London: H. F. & G. Witherby, 1924–1939. Reprinted by Barnes and Noble, Inc., New York, N. Y., 1960–1961.

Baker, Ernest A. and Packman, James. *Guide to Historical Fiction.* New York: The Macmillan Company, 1914.

Baker, Ernest A. and Packman, James. *Guide to the Best Fiction.* New York: The Macmillan Company, 1932.

Coan, O. W. and Lillard, R. G. *America in Fiction.* Stanford University, Calif.: Stanford University Press, 5th edition, 1967.
List of novels on various aspects of American life.

Cook, Dorothy E. and Fidell, Estella A. *Fiction Catalog.* New York: H. W. Wilson Company, 7th edition, 1960. Annual supplements.

Cook, Dorothy E. and Monro, Isabel S. *Short Story Index.* New York: H. W. Wilson Company, 1953. Supplements, 1956, 1960.
Supersedes Firkins, I. T. E., *Index to Short Stories.* 60,000 stories indexed by author, title, and subject.

Eastman, Mary Huse. *Index to Fairy Tales, Myths, and Legends.* Boston, Mass.: F. W. Faxon Company, 1926. Supplements, 1937, 1952.

Poetry.

Granger, Edith. *Index to Poetry.* New York: Columbia University Press, 5th edition, 1962. Suppl. edition, 1967.

HISTORY (Library Number 900)

Biographical Dictionaries of Famous People.

Appleton's Cyclopaedia of American Biography. 7 vols. New York: D. Appleton and Company, 1887-1900.
Arrangement: alphabetical, with index.

New Century Cyclopedia of Names. 3 vols. New York: Appleton-Century-Crofts, 1954.

Chambers's Biographical Dictionary. New York: St. Martin's Press, new edition, 1961, 1962.

Dictionary of American Biography. 21 vols. New York: Charles Scribner's Sons, 1928-1937. Reprinted 1943, 1946 (11 vols.)
Biographies of famous Americans who have made some "original contribution to American life." Arrangement: alphabetical.

Dictionary of National Biography. New York: Oxford University Press, 1882-1900. Supplements to 1950.
Biographies of famous people of the British Empire. Arrangement: alphabetical, with supplements, indexes, and epitomes. *Concise Dictionary of National Biography,* an Epitomé and Supplement in 2 vols., 1953.

Kunitz, Stanley J. and Haycraft, Howard. *British Authors of the Nineteenth Century.* New York: H. W. Wilson Company, 1936.

Kunitz, Stanley J. and Haycraft, Howard. *Twentieth Century Authors.* New York: H. W. Wilson Company, 1942, Supplement, 1955.

National Cyclopedia of American Biography. New York: James T. White and Company, 1892-1957. 43 vols.

Webster's Biographical Dictionary. Springfield, Mass.: G. & C. Merriam Company, 1964.
Brief biographies of 40,000 people of all centuries and from every field.

Biographical Dictionaries of Living and Recent People.

Who's Who. London: A. & C. Black, Ltd., 1849 to date.
Annual volumes. Concise information about living Englishmen and a few people of other nations. *Who Was Who* is a periodic supplement.

Who's Who in America. Chicago: A. N. Marquis Company, 1899 to date.
Biennial volumes. Monthly supplements.

Who Was Who in America. Chicago: A. N. Marquis Company. Vol. 1 (1897-1942), 1942; Vol. 2 (1943-1950), 1950.

The list of books on the *Who's Who* principle is too long to be given in full. The following titles may be helpful to those seeking information in special fields.

Authors.

American Women Poets; Authors of Today; Authors of Today and Yesterday; British Authors before 1800; Who's Who among North American Authors; Who's Who in Literature; The Book of Authors.

Classes or Professions.

American Men of Science; Directory of American Scholars; Leaders in Education; Who's Who among: Physicians and Surgeons; Women Lawyers; Who's Who in American Art; American Education; American Government; the Army; Art; Aviation; British Science; Broadcasting; Commerce and Industry; Dancing; Economics; Engineering; Insurance; Labor; Law; Library Service; Sports; the Theatre; Transportation and Communication.

Localities.

Chi é? (Italian); Qui Etes-vous? (French); Thom's Irish Who's Who: Wer Ist's (German); Who's Who in: Australia; Austria; British Columbia; Canada; Central and East Europe; China; Egypt; France; India, Burma, and Ceylon; Israel; Italy; Japan; Latin America; New Zealand; the Philippines; Spain; Switzerland; Wales.

Who's Who in: the East; the Midwest; New England; New York; the South and the Southwest; the West.

Music.

American Composers Today; Composers of Yesterday; European Composers Today; International Who's Who in Music; Musicians' Guide; Who's Who among Southern Singers and Composers; Who's Who Today in the Musical World.

Other Fields.

American Women; America's Young Men; Italian-American Who's Who; Who Knows—and What; Woman's Who's Who of America; Who's Who in American Jewry; Who's Who in Colored America; Who's Who in the United Nations; Who's Who in United States Politics and American Political Almanac.

Many universities publish alumni directories giving brief factual accounts of their graduates. These are generally available in university libraries.

Classical Antiquities.

Cary, M., ed. *Oxford Classical Dictionary.* New York: Oxford University Press, 1949.

Peck, Harry T. *Harper's Dictionary of Classical Literature and Antiquities.* New York: Harper and Brothers, 1897.

General History.

For histories, manuals, source books, and bibliographies on special periods or countries, see Winchell, *Guide to Reference Books.* For American history see also *Harvard Guide to American History,* edited by Oscar Handlin and others, published by Harvard University Press, 1954.

American Historical Association. *Guide to Historical Literature.* Edited by George F. Howe. New York: The Macmillan Company, 1961.

Hockett, Homer C. *The Critical Method in Historical Research and Writing.* New York: The Macmillan Company, 1955.

International Bibliography of Historical Sciences. New York: H. W. Wilson Company. 1930 to date.
    Annotated and classified list of historical publications.

Keller, Helen R. *Dictionary of Dates.* 2 vols. New York: The Macmillan Company, 1934.

Langer, William L., ed. *Encyclopedia of World History.* Boston, Mass.: Houghton Mifflin Company, revised edition, 1952.
    A revised and enlarged edition of *Ploetz' Manual of Universal History.*

Larned, Josephus N. *New Larned History for Ready Reference.* Springfield, Mass.: Nichols Press, 1922-1924.
    Alphabetical dictionary of world history, with cross references. Each article is quoted from some recognized authority. Thus the work constitutes an index to histories.

Little, Charles E. *Historical Lights.* New York: Funk and Wagnalls Company, 1892.
    Six thousand quotations from famous histories and biographies. An index enables one to find material about subjects or people.

Morris, Richard B., ed. *Encyclopedia of American History.* New York: Harper and Brothers, revised edition, 1965.

Syrett, Harold C., ed. *American Historical Documents.* New York: Barnes and Noble, Inc., 1960.

CHAPTER THREE

Preliminary Evaluation of Material

Evaluate your bibliography as collected. Eliminate works that you will not use, noting on the card for each relinquished title why the work is not helpful. Make a brief study of each remaining work, according to the leading queries in this chapter.

The Problem of Evaluation. "Meek young men grow up in libraries, believing it their duty to accept the views which Cicero, which Locke, which Bacon, have given; forgetful that Cicero, Locke, and Bacon were only young men in libraries when they wrote these books." Thus Emerson in his famous lecture called "The American Scholar" expressed the duty of evaluating what one reads. But how are you, young, no expert yourself, to sit in judgment upon the great and learned of the earth, and estimate the adequacy of their work? Obviously, you will get nowhere by following mere hit-or-miss first impressions which allow free play for your own bias and ignorance. Here are a few guides to help in carrying out the heavy responsibility of thinking for yourself among the able, deliberate, learned thinkers in books.

PRIMARY AND SECONDARY SOURCES

Is the Document in Question a Primary Source or a Secondary Source of Information for Your Purpose? A primary source is a direct, first-hand document. If you write about a book, the book itself is your main primary source. An eye witness, a personal acquaintance of a person written about, the doer of a thing—all such people are in a position to be primary sources of information. The value of any account depends upon the primary sources from which it is taken. If those sources are unreliable, later accounts will inherit the original unreliability. All research, therefore, in delving for truth, is to some extent a study of sources. What did Shakespeare actually write, in a disputed passage? What did the inventor himself say that he was trying to discover? For centuries scholars had guessed and wondered about the death of Christopher Marlowe. Theories and legends were available, but none was reliable. But when Leslie Hotson discovered a contemporary document telling the story of Marlowe's death, that testimony of actual observers cleared away much insubstantial guesswork.

Those who are not accustomed to the ways of research may not at first consideration be attracted to primary sources. Those documents often appear, and are, disreputable or incompetent. What Shakespeare actually wrote, if it could be discovered at all, might not seem so metrical or so sensible as something that ingenious guessing editors have suggested. A half-literate first-hand account of a battle may seem less plausible than an expert's theoretical reconstruction of the event. It is often a great pity that some of our important primary sources are not more reliable. But we do not remedy the matter by altering them. And our ablest, most eloquent interpretations of them are after all less authoritative than the bare, imperfect documents themselves. The only way to improve the situation is to discover new primary sources to correct and supplement those that we have. But, in the nature of the case, that cannot often be done. Therefore we have to make the best of existing primary sources, realizing their unique value and their painful limitations.

The value of secondary sources depends largely upon the accuracy with which they record their findings, upon the acuteness of their interpretations and evaluations, upon the validity of their reasoning, upon the usefulness of their conclusions and applications. For facts, therefore, a secondary document is an inferior, though perhaps highly reliable source. For interpretation and application such a document may be very helpful. But on the other hand it may mislead you or tempt you to become a mere parrot.

THE WRITER

Does the Writer Have First-Hand Knowledge of His Subject? If he lived at the time, among the persons and events he describes, that fact gives his word a certain weight. He may be lying. He may be an incompetent witness. But as one who saw, he is a first-hand witness. He has a right to speak. His writing is a primary source, a first source, because he stood at the fountain-head of truth in that matter.

Does the Writer Have the Reputation of Being a Reliable Scholar? Look him up, in a good encyclopedia if he can be found there; in *Who's Who* if he is still alive. What are his degrees, official positions, experiences, publications; and how do they bear upon what he has written? As for his writings, look up competent criticisms and reviews of them. Encyclopedias and various special works evaluate the books of older writers. The *A.L.A. Booklist* or the *Book Review Digest* serve for late books. The judgment of these reviews and criticisms is not final. You may find pronouncements that disagree with other expert opinions in the matter. Nevertheless your findings do have a certain weight in evaluating the works you will use. Reputation, even in this field of supposedly objective scholarship, may be misleading, but it is not therefore negligible.

Is the Writer Biased? Does he *seem* biased? Do his origin, experience, reputation, or present circumstances suggest the probability of bias? A rich man, for instance, may be biased against socialism, or a member of an oppressed race may hate the oppressors. An advocate of a theory may see little good in those who oppose his theory. The question of bias is not simple. There are degrees of bias. There is probably unconscious prejudice in some who proclaim and believe in their own fairness. There is subtle bias, hard to detect, but a real influence in bringing writers to certain conclusions. A known bias does not necessarily invalidate a person's argument or his conclusions, but it throws doubt upon them and lessens their influence with readers.

THE WORK ITSELF

What Is Implied in the Date of a Work? A newspaper of a certain day in 1870 states that a fire occurred on that day. A witness of that fire, who wrote about it years later, gives a different date. A historian, writing still later, gives, on his own unsupported word, a third date for the fire. Any one of these dates may be right. Or all may be wrong. But on the face of the matter, the newspaper is the best authority, because of its date, which gives the writer less chance to forget, or to be misled as to the day.

On the other hand, an American newspaper which printed lurid stories of German atrocities in 1917, is an unreliable authority, because of the date. For we now know that during the war the press was misinformed in such matters, and was extremely biased. A historian's account written twenty years later would be more likely to come near the truth.

A pre-war geography of Europe, a 1920 treatise on aviation are now to a great extent out of date. An eighteenth-century opinion of Shakespeare is not likely to be accepted in our day.

Thus it is clear that old writings are not necessarily better or worse than later ones. They have different values, different uses. Only when you have decided what use you would make of a document, can you rightly estimate the effect of its date. But once the use has been determined, the date helps materially in setting your evaluation upon the document.

Does the Publisher, or the Periodical in Which the Work Appears, Suggest Bias? Newspapers of some countries are censored by their government. American newspapers may have to express the views of their owners or political sponsors. Some publications are supported by a church, a university, or a private foundation, which may or may not dictate what shall be published and how. The control exercised may be complete and arbitrary or lax and negligible, and its significance varies. When a Republican newspaper praises the Democrats, its praise is more significant than propaganda in a Democratic newspaper. But when a

Republican journal finds fault with some Democratic policy, the possibility that this criticism is sheer bias detracts from its force. Books and magazines also may follow the prejudices of their publishers.

In evaluating a work, then, consider what you know about the publisher. Make allowance for any commitment or bias that this consideration may suggest.

What Is the Opinion of Critics concerning the Work in Question? Is the work recommended in the selected bibliographies of encyclopedias and other standard reference books? Is it favorably reviewed? (See *Book Review Digest* and *A.L.A. Booklist.* These serve for books, but critical opinion on periodical studies is generally not easily available.) In the criticisms and evaluations which you find, what seem to be the qualities for which the work is recommended? Is it said to have other qualities, which you should beware of?

Does Your First Inspection of the Work Itself Suggest Some Tentative Appraisals of Its Probable Value for Your Purpose? Does the scope of the work, as revealed on the title page and in the table of contents, offer more or less than you need? Does the preface disclose anything regarding the author's sources or purposes (serious? unbiased?) that should affect your use of the work? Do chapter analyses or marginal summaries mention topics that may be useful to you? Does the index show material or topics that concern you?

As you dip into the work here and there, do you find evidence of bad thinking? Do the statements and conclusions seem credible, reasonable, reconcilable with common sense? Do you suspect wish thinking, a tendency to arrive at desired conclusions in spite of evidence to the contrary? Is there a sentimental tendency to overestimate the value of some facts simply because they are agreeable to the author? Do you notice any lack of thoroughness, omission of important considerations, or imperfect statements of fact? Do you suspect credulity in acceptance of statistics or opinions? Do the author's reasoning processes seem unreliable, perhaps just on certain subjects, such as nationality, race, party, creed, philosophical or economic theory, youth, age, illness? Is there exaggeration, obsession, unscrupulousness, personal meanness, professional enmity, a tendency to belittle or ridicule those who disagree, or a tendency to serve self-interest and reputation? These latter traits should certainly be noted. A work may be valuable in spite of them, but they tend to detract from its weight and render it suspect.

Does the Documentation Seem Adequate in Quantity and Quality? As you read along, ask yourself how the writer knows the matters he is relating. Unless he expresses only his personal opinion, or facts which he has himself observed, his knowledge must have come through some media. Of course he may write of well-known and undisputed facts. It is not necessary to cite an authority for the statement that football is a game which involves running. But when the facts are less well known, and especially when they are disputable, they require documentation. Direct quotations, statistics, thoughts or acts imputed to people beyond the writer's personal observation, all require careful and detailed reference to the source of the information. Works in which such references are not given may have value for some popular purpose, but they are imperfectly adapted to research study.

An author's statement can hardly be more reliable than its source. Therefore the source must be trustworthy, and it must cover the points for which it is cited. It must be cited fairly. Sentences should not be taken out of their context so as to alter their meaning. Any tampering with sources or misinterpreting of them should be noted. Of course you cannot be expected to verify the footnotes, but if you happen to notice any shortcomings as you glance over the pages, such observations have an obvious bearing upon the work in hand.

SUGGESTIONS FOR STUDY

Consider the bibliography on pages 155-157. From the titles and descriptions of the various works, estimate which ones contain primary sources. Which two of these works would you consider off-hand the most important sources for the essay? In the case of what works in the list can you feel confident that the writer had first-hand knowledge of his subject? Consider the probable scholarship of the writers of secondary works in the list. Can you find any evidences that might seem to indicate scholarly standing or reputation? Do you notice any probability of bias?

Consider the footnotes in the documented paper on pages 106-157. Which ones are based directly upon primary sources? Do you find any footnote references that are weakened by the date of the source cited?

CHAPTER FOUR

Reading and Taking Notes

Take classified notes on your reading. Use the methods suggested in this chapter.

THE USE OF NOTE CARDS

Take your notes on cards. It is handy to use the same three-by-five cards that serve for bibliography. Some prefer the four-by-six size. The larger cards afford more space for long notes, but they are more expensive and more cumbersome, more wasteful of space when notes are short. Plan not to be without cards at your studies. Temporary notes in notebooks or on backs of envelopes can be, in a way, worse than no notes, for they promote confusion.

Write plainly and accurately, without crowding. Do not count on copying your notes. Get them right the first time. Copying only opens the way for more mistakes.

Use the upper left-hand corner of the card for the subject heading of the note. As soon as possible, organize all your subject headings of notes into a system to correspond with parts of the outline for your essay. Many notes classified under a few subject headings promote orderly progress. Multiplicity of subject headings leads to confusion.

Write upon only one topic on a card. If a note must be long, it may occupy several properly numbered and identified cards. Most scholars have no scruple against using both sides of cards.

Just *below* the note itself, state the source, clearly and accurately, by author, work, and page (line number is better than page number for poetry having numbered lines, since a line-number reference serves for any edition). Do not use drastic abbreviations or code symbols in this reference. Your corresponding bibliography card will give complete data for the document cited, but the reference on the reading note should be sufficient in itself, even years after it is made.

It is very important, if you are to achieve an independent study, that the note cards should be classified by their subject headings, at the top; not by their sources, at the bottom. Classification by sources leads to docile following of an organization that others have handed down to you. Classification by your own subject headings makes easier your task of imposing an original form upon your study. It is for this reason that you should put the source reference at the bottom of the card, where it is least likely to have undue influence upon your plan of organization.

KINDS OF NOTES

Outline Notes. A note may be in the form of an outline, covering either a whole article or some part of it. Care should be taken to make sure that the requirements of the outline form do not warp the actual discussion represented.

Academic satire in _Alice_ books
    Students
        Tweedledum, -dee
    Alumni
        Gryphon, Mock Turtle
    Faculty
        Hatter, March Hare, White King,
        Lion, Unicorn, Humpty Dumpty,
        White Knight

        Ayres, H. M. "Lewis Carroll and
      the 'Alice' Books." _Columbia_
      Univ. Quar., vol. 24, pp. 170-173.

Notice with what modifications the material from this sample card is used on page 142.

Summary and Paraphrase Notes. The summary may cover either all or part of the work in question. It may omit matters irrelevant to your subject, or to the topic that you put at the top of the card. Of course it must be true to the word and spirit of the work you are reading. A paraphrase is expressed in your words, not in the author's, and any of the author's language used should be put in quotation marks. Since a paraphrase does not condense to the same extent as a summary, it usually covers only a brief passage. It is handier than quotation, wherever the author's words are not exactly suitable for your purpose. You should not misinterpret the author's ideas in your rephrasing.

In paraphrases or summaries, since you use your own words, abbreviations and other short cuts are permissible. But these should be consistent, and so simple that they will still be intelligible to you after the notes are cold.

```
Alice L. autographs Wonderland
     Autographs a copy for Princess Eliza-
beth.  Only copy, it is believed, she
ever autographed.
                    N.Y.Times, Ap. 19, 1932,
                    p. 19, col. 8.
```

The material on this sample card is used on page 153.

Quotation Notes. When you quote a writer's own words, enclose them in quotation marks. Quote exactly, even to punctuation and vagaries in grammar or spelling. The expression *sic* may indicate mistakes for which the writer quoted is responsible. Indicate omissions in quoted matter by three dots (. . .) where words have been left out. If you add any words of your own in a quoted passage, enclose them in square brackets. Do not use quotation marks for indirect quotations, or for anything stated in your own words.

Direct quotation is helpful when: (1) the point is very important; (2) the matter is something to be refuted; (3) the statement concerned is ambiguous; (4) there is a chance that your citation may be called in question; (5) the point is so well or characteristically stated that the very style will be an advantage in your paper. You should perhaps take down more quotations than you expect to use, and record in full some of the passages from which you may finally select only a few words. The opportunity for choice and the background of context may prove helpful.

> Carroll on Alice L., 1885
>
> "My mental picture is as vivid as ever of one who was, through so many years, my ideal child-friend. I have had scores of child-friends since your time, but they have been quite a different thing."
>
> Collingwood, Life, p. 237.

The use of the material from this note will be found on page 141. The reference, however, is not there necessary, for the emphasis is upon the other "child-friends," who are described more fully elsewhere in the Collingwood biography.

Commentary Notes. Comments may take various forms: e.g., queries, comparisons, criticisms of fact or argument, ideas for using or developing certain points, notes locating maps or diagrams. It is important to put down such ideas as they occur to you, for you may otherwise forget them when you set about writing your paper.

> Tenniel's animals
>
> Carroll had the wrong idea in using the natural histories for animals. Walt Disney looks in the glass. Tenniel's animals are more human. See lion and unicorn. Are they French and English? They fight for the crown.
>
> Looking-Glass, p. 230.

The material on this card, like a great deal that goes down in card notes, was finally not needed. Yet it is such commentary notes that sometimes develop into the most original and valuable features of a study.

THE THESIS AND THE CLASSIFICATION OF NOTES

When you begin your reading, you face a dilemma. If you have a clear goal set for your study, and a plan of development worked out, you do not begin with an open mind. Your project in that case is not true research, a quest for truth, but a more or less elaborate justification of ideas, perhaps prejudices, held to begin with. On the other hand, if you begin, as you should, with no unchangeable goal or plan, you may well find yourself at a loss about what to look for, what notes to take.

It is almost inevitable, then, that your notes will do little but outline or summarize the first few documents you study. Then when you have seen something of the conclusions reached by others and the steps by which they have reached them, you may begin to conceive a goal and plan of your own. Your plan should not be the same as that some other writer has followed, unless you feel that you can add to or correct his work. And if you assume a task of enlargement and correction, you should only briefly restate what your predecessor has done. You should emphasize your original contribution. As research, your work must undertake an original focus of facts toward a purpose not elsewhere so specifically adopted. Indeed, this need for an original plan is what makes research something more than a mere clerk's job of copying and filing. And the plan, once made, will thereafter determine what notes you will take and under what headings you will classify them.

First, let us suppose, you conceive a goal for your study. You want to show, perhaps, that Benjamin Franklin made some noteworthy contributions to physical education. This is a vague objective, but it may be soon clarified. When you have listed Franklin's accomplishments in physical education, you will look for the status of physical education at his time, and for the effects of his work upon later developments. So your objective may become much more specific. You may be able to state it by filling out such a formula as: since Benjamin Franklin's interest and achievements in physical education included . . . , and because his influence led to . . ., he should have the credit for . . . This kind of statement, which forms a nucleus for your whole subsequent study, is called a thesis.

Note the form which the thesis statement takes. It is one sentence, simple or complex, but not compound. A compound sentence, or several simple sentences, might leave some doubt as to which part contains the focus of thought. Such statements are scattering. It is the function of the thesis to give your study unity—one purpose, one goal. To do this, a complex sentence is very apt. The subordinate clauses, which should come first, indicate or imply the steps by which the goal is approached; finally the independent clause states the goal. Thus you indicate the essay's focus, not merely by the point to be reached, but by the lines of thought along which you move to reach it. Such a statement implies the main headings for the outline of your essay. So in the case of the Franklin essay, you might have as headings:

> Opinions and practices in physical education during Franklin's day.

> Franklin's interests and accomplishments in physical education.

> Franklin's influence upon later developments in this field.

A few examples will show how specific theses imply outlines for different essay structures.

Thesis: Since cats fit into different types of domestication without changing themselves so much as dogs do, the modern cat is more primitive than the modern dog.

> *Outline:* Examples of adaptation by cats without much change in nature or habits.

> Examples of adaptation by dogs, involving great changes in nature and habits.

> Comparison of modern with primitive cats, showing only superficial differences.
>
> Comparison of modern with primitive dogs, showing greater differences.

Thesis: Though adaptation of educational procedures to the age levels of children makes school more humane than it used to be, the modern project of educating even the barely educable has kept the total of child suffering very high.

> *Outline:* Examples of oldtime child sufferings, due to procedures unfit for the age level at which they were used.
>
> Examples of modern child sufferings, due to unfitness of certain children for the educational program prescribed.
>
> Statistics showing the number and proportion of children affected at the two periods covered.

Thesis: Although corpses were a standard requirement in the Gothic romance of Poe's day, Poe shows in his life and in his stories an obsession with corpses that was more personal and pathological than the convention called for.

> *Outline:* Examples and statistics showing to what extent corpses were used in Gothic romances not by Poe.
>
> Examples and statistics showing the particularly morbid use of corpses in Poe's stories.
>
> Aspects of Poe's life and character which seem to confirm the pathological nature of the obsession with corpses.

An attentive consideration of these examples should show how crucial a thesis is. With a good thesis properly stated, the problem of organization is to a large extent solved.

But you must clearly understand the difference between a thesis, adopted to give your study direction, and a prejudice or preconceived idea which would make your work only so much special pleading. A thesis is at first a hypothesis, something to be developed, established *if possible*. But a true researcher will modify his thesis as he goes along, if necessary, to fit his findings after maturer study. You must not become too much committed to your thesis. At first it is only something to try. Your loyalty is not to this temporary experiment, but only to the truth. Get a thesis, then, and go to work on it. If you find, upon reading further, that it is wrong, abandon it. If you find that it is imperfectly stated, modify it. This process of adaptation to the facts is in general the essence of the very successful modern method of study which has in the last century gone far to reshape civilization.

CHAPTER FIVE

Organization of Material

Examine the following methods and devices. Select the method or combination of methods best suited to your study in hand, and proceed to organize your material accordingly.

THE IMPORTANCE OF PROPER METHODS IN RESEARCH

The general outlines of acceptable research methods are essential for advanced study, and therefore it is best to learn and practice them now, though with limited scope and precision. Even though these methods are imperfectly carried out, they may give your present work a value that it would not otherwise have.

There are three accepted methods of organizing research material with scientific validity: the normative, the experimental, the historical. Some other methods may be valid for unpretentious studies, but would not alone serve all the purposes of strict research. In most research, a combination of methods is used.

THE NORMATIVE METHOD

The normative method is concerned with the question, "What is best?" Sometimes this involves or is equivalent to such questions as: "What is true? What is the average, or the rule? What works? What is preferred?" Deeply human, the issue is a matter of values. Government, economics, philosophy, religion, the arts try to establish norms or averages or standards for the changing world, and to keep those precarious norms up to date. Sometimes simple statistics are needed, for such matters as population, production, or legislation. Sometimes weighted statistics are used, as in politics by voting, in education by tests, in medicine by physical

examinations. The weighted statistics measure facts in some relation to objectives. Sometimes we can put two and two together
and infer that a certain attempted remedy did work (like vac-
cination for smallpox) or did not work (like prohibition). But
the facts change while we reason, and the valid norm which worked
yesterday becomes an anachronism today. Nevertheless our findings
are often the best guide we have, ever so much better than guesswork or blind faith in some traditional formula.

The so-called normative sciences (including especially the
applied parts of any subject of study) proceed by a process of
finding and interpreting the relevant facts, deciding upon a desired
result, finding means that may produce that result, trying those
means, and then, if they work, applying them upon as large a
scale as possible. This process could be illustrated in law, medicine,
engineering, education, politics, and many other fields. Only the
first three steps of the process are likely to concern your elementary research.

Finding and Interpreting the Facts. Some facts it is
comparatively simple, though often expensive and time-consuming,
to find, as for example the population of a country. It is more
difficult to discover the distance of remote stars. Some things,
however, we have never learned to measure or count. Our groping
intelligence tests have made progress, but, so far, no one is quite
satisfied with these attempts to measure intelligence. Publishers
would be glad if they knew how to measure the appeal of the
books they intend to issue. Historians, after the fact, can only
guess how much a song or a speech or a cartoon had to do with
the issue of a certain election. Statistics, then, in these fields, are
not so helpful as are the data of the "exact" sciences like physics
or chemistry. Yet some statistics are available, whatever their
bearing, and the reward, often, of pondering them, is great for any
one who can find a valid interpretation.

An interpretation of statistics is considered valid if it squares
with other generalizations that have gained acceptance by working,
and if its implications lead to predictions that can be regularly

77

fulfilled. We should welcome an aptitude test, for example, which could predict a student's success in college as well as astronomers predict an eclipse.

For your present purposes, you will probably not do much actual counting or measuring. The figures and facts that you use, you will doubtless find in books: histories, atlases, yearbooks, almanacs, encyclopedias, government statistics, and similar works. Much interpretation of these data will also be available in books. So most of the spadework is already done for you, perhaps far more extensively and accurately than you would ever be able to do it. But still your task is far from simple. The use of statistics is a very complicated art in itself. Just what do the figures mean? How do they apply to your particular problem? Without a clear head and a mastery of some rather complicated mathematics, you can easily go wrong in answering these questions. Mathematics, however, is only extended common sense. You may use figures with impunity in as far as you understand them and the processes which govern them. Like high-voltage wires, they are not to be handled indiscriminately by the ignorant. The following principles may guide you:

In your original applications of statistics, be sure that you know the meaning of the figures, and the technique of any processes which you use in applying them. (You need to know the meaning of terms used. What is an intelligence quotient, for example? Do you understand something of its validity, implications, uses?)

In citing the statistical studies of others, be sure to state your source. This will not only give credit where it is due; it will also clear you of responsibility for inaccuracies in the work of others.

Deciding upon a Desired Result. Deciding what we want, though it seems easy at first, is harder and less scientific than getting and evaluating statistics. Yet relative desirableness of alternative issues can be carefully estimated, and measurements can be taken (as in voting), though the desirableness itself at present evades us. We have to be as careful and accurate as we can.

Finding of Means That May Produce the Desired Result.

As long as you remain in the stage of merely proposing measures, this task of proposing seems easier than it is. But you cannot be content merely to convince yourself and your friends. Your proposals are tested finally by the twisting chances of complicated, inexorable reality. You are exceptionally lucky, or your work is really sound, if your proposed measures stand that test.

But the normative method, for all its imperfections, has its great advantages. Especially: it is interesting; and its results may be, for a time at least, practical.[1]

THE EXPERIMENTAL METHOD

Experiment is controlled observation. You may control practically all the phenomena, as when the delicate apparatus of laboratories is fully applicable. Or you may control only a few important circumstances, as when astronomers study an eclipse from carefully selected positions, at particular times, with a purposeful variety of instruments.

You can use the experimental method as the means and pattern for a whole research task. Or it may merely contribute a detail in the execution of a project that follows, in the main, some other method. Not all experiments are so formal and accurate as those carried on with great care by scientists. Business experiments are frequently undertaken to locate favorable sites for markets or offices. Social experiments by boards and commissions try out proposed measures and report the degree of success or failure. Soundings with questionnaires, trials of budget plans, variations

---

1 The foregoing discussion of the normative method has not included scientific devices for finding and proving the validity of norms. For deriving norms, various score cards, scales, and tests have been found satisfactory in some projects. The so-called Pearson coefficient of correlation, and other similar formulae, are useful in testing the validity of a norm or measuring device. Students who are interested and who have the requisite mathematical background are referred for further information to the following works.

Herbert Arkin and Raymond R. Colton, *Statistical Methods* (4th ed.; New York: Barnes and Noble, Inc., revised 1956).

Herbert Arkin and Raymond R. Colton, *Tables for Statisticians* (2nd ed.; New York: Barnes and Noble, Inc., 1963).

J. P. Guilford, *Fundamental Statistics in Psychology and Education* (4th ed.; New York: McGraw-Hill Book Company, 1965).

of election methods, and countless similar activities may sometimes be classified as experiments. Experiments are also possible in books. You may test passages, at random or by some method of selection, for definite qualities of style. Thus by metrical tests some help was brought to the task of dating Shakespeare's plays. Or you may go through books to get and compare attitudes or information regarding certain topics. By varying your procedure, you can produce the necessary amount of control to make your activity a genuine experiment. Such experiments do not always yield trustworthy results, for the conditions are only imperfectly controlled, and accidental factors may invalidate any conclusions drawn. But neither are these imperfect experiments worthless in general. If the control is sufficient in relevant matters, and if enough experiments are brought to bear upon a problem, valuable findings may result.

The headings for reporting a scientific experiment are fairly standardized:

> Presentation of the general field or topic of the experimentation.
>
> Hypothesis.
>
> Subjects experimented upon.
>
> Apparatus described and, if necessary, drawn.
>
> Procedure in the experiment.
>
> Data accumulated.
>
> Resulting generalizations.
>
> Relation of all this to the general field or general theory.

The same general form, though perhaps less rigid, and with appropriate adaptations, may serve for any sort of experimental study.[1]

---

1 The detailed techniques of scientific experiment are too complicated for our present discussion, or for your use in this assignment. This is particularly true of the mathematics and logic by which the results of experimentation are brought to bear upon various situations. Interested students are referred to the following works for further information.

W. I. B. Beveridge, *Art of Scientific Investigation* (New York: W. W. Norton Company, rev. ed., 1957).

H. Poincaré, *Science and Hypothesis* (New York: Dover Publications, Inc., 1952).
H. Poincaré, *Science and Method* (New York: Dover Publications, Inc., 1952).

THE HISTORICAL METHOD

The historical method follows, or at least takes into careful account, the order of chronology and development. The method is not peculiar to political history. Everything, including each science and each method of study, has its causes, origin, history, development. Therefore any subject may be studied by the historical method, though some other method may be better for a particular purpose. The commonest materials of historical study are books and documents. Therefore for such work you should be an unusually able reader. You may have to cover a great deal of hard reading, and yet be answerable for accuracy in nice details. All the problems of evaluating sources and taking notes are prominent in historical work.

The organization of material follows the order of cause and effect, which must be basically chronological.

> Causes.
> Origin.
> Successive steps of development.
> Results.
> Conclusions or generalizations from the study.

Frequently the whole discussion is preceded by a statement of the thesis, or hypothesis, of the study, which must be borne out in the conclusion.

It should be noted that the chronological order is not alone a sufficient method. The succession of events means little unless it follows a causal series and unless that series leads to an enlightening, worth-while conclusion.[1]

---

1 References on the historical method:
    H. Ausubel, *Historians and Their Craft* (New York: Russell and Russell, Inc., 1965).
    C. L. Becker, *Everyman His Own Historian* (New York: Appleton-Century-Crofts, Inc., 1948).
    W. P. Gee, *Social Science Research Methods* (New York: Appleton-Century-Crofts, Inc., 1950).
    H. C. Hockett, *Critical Method in Historical Research and Writing* (3rd ed. of *Introduction to Research in American History* (New York: The Macmillan Company, 1955).
    G. J. Renier, *History: Its Purpose and Method* (Boston, Mass.: Beacon Press, 1950).

OTHER METHODS AND DEVICES INCIDENTAL
TO RESEARCH

The Case Study. One can make an extensive study of one book, of one episode or experience, of one patient in a clinic, of one law case, of one engineering project, or of any single, limited problem. Such a study may be very thorough, for the field is comparatively small. It may be very enlightening, for it is likely that no one else has gone so thoroughly into the individual problem. It need not be narrow, for the principles and backgrounds involved may be very extensive, no matter how limited the immediate problem. One sort of case study is chronological and developmental, using parts of the historical method. Another sort is some kind of interview or inspection. Case studies are inspiring to a beginner, for the task seems fresh, and all his own. As a step in a larger project which includes many cases, such a study may be a legitimate part of scientific research. But as a thing in itself, a case study is incomplete. No conclusions can be validly drawn from one case. If the task is furnished with conclusions or a diagnosis, there is implied a larger study, without which the conclusions must be guesswork. So when a thorough review of a book ends by appraising it as an example of its age or type, we have to assume that the reviewer has qualified himself as a judge of other writings implied in such a comparison. Therefore the case-study method will not alone serve for an adanced research project.

The Genetic Method. .A genetic study traces the development of its subject, stressing the causal sequence of events. If this development involves stages not directly observed by the student, the study is really a limited example of the historical method. The evolutionary development of an animal through past ages could be so studied. If the development can be fully observed and its changes controlled, the study is essentially experimental. If enough cases are included to afford valid norms, the method may become normative. But any genetic study which lacks one of these extensions of method, is insufficiently sound and complete for proper research. Where direct observation or relevant documenta-

82

tion is lacking, the data are likely to be incomplete. Where past events are concerned, verification of observation is generally impossible, for one does not have the multiple testimony available in the larger field of history. However, genetic studies are of value when they are carried on in combination with other methods.

The Comparative Method. The normative method involves comparison, but by elaborate mathematical analysis of the statistics concerned, the norms may be given a very exact, often useful and versatile meaning. Simpler, naive comparisons, like comparative scores of football teams, may have no certain meaning. Tables ranking things in regard to various qualities and affording a comparison of the rankings have the value of making simple relationships clear. But the story they seem to tell may not be true. In short, comparisons may convince, but they seldom prove. They should be subjected to careful analysis and used with caution.

The Survey Method. By surveying a certain field for statistics, one can get material for case studies or for comparisons. One might get enough statistics to supply scientific norms. Wherever that is done, the method is really normative. Otherwise, the survey method is only an elaboration or combination of case study and comparison. It has the same characteristics that were noted of them.

Compilation. A compilation of original sources (primary material) or of material from them is a handy instrument for research. It may be a necessary preliminary to research. But by itself it lacks the achievement of original conclusions which proper research must have. A compilation of secondary sources or of their material is a task for criticism, not for research. Opinions or conclusions which other scholars have reached regarding your subject may be suggestive and helpful to you. Or they may be misleading and conflicting. But in any case they are not the data upon which you as a researcher should build. Though cognizant of them, you do your work with those sources which are closest to the facts themselves. Compilation, then, as a method in research, is only incidental.

The Questionnaire. Questionnaires are not in good repute as a device for research. They are convenient or necessary sometimes when needed information is scattered widely or located in very distant places. Results of actual questionnaires have not generally stood validation well or proved very reliable. Generally not more than half of the people who receive forms answer them at all. Those who do answer are sometimes careless or facetious in what they set down. But if the data can be verified and the results validated, the device may be helpfully used with the normative method.[1]

---

1 List of references on supplementary devices in research:
  D. H. Fryer and E. R. Henry, *Handbook of Applied Psychology* (New York: Rinehart and Company, 1950).
  C. V. Good, *Introduction to Educational Research* (2nd ed.; New York: Appleton-Century-Crofts, Inc., 1962).
  F. B. Loomis, *The Evolution of the Horse* (Boston, Mass.: Marshall Jones, 1926). An example of the genetic method.
  G. A. Lundbery, "Case Work and the Statistical Method," *Social Forces*, XLV (September, 1925), 61-65.
  Frederick L. Whitney, *Elements of Research* (3rd ed.; New York: Prentice-Hall, Inc., 1950).

CHAPTER SIX

The Outline

Make a sentence outline for your proposed essay Follow the instructions in this chapter.

For sample outlines, see pages 89 and 104.

Your Method of Organizing Material Affects Your Outline. With the help of your thesis and its implications, you have already classified your reading notes by headings that imply a simple preliminary outline. However, the method which you have followed in further organizing your notes may suggest some modification of your original headings. For instance, the normative method suggests dividing the material into three groups:

The facts.
The desired results.
Means for achieving those results.

The experimental and historical methods also conduce to their own typical outline divisions, as will be seen by referring to the preceding chapter.

The Outline Form. The System of Numbers, Letters, and Indentation. Once the main divisions are roughly blocked out, an experimental skeleton outline may be made with properly numbered and lettered parts. There should not be too minute a subdivision. Follow this system:

I ....

   A ....

   B ....

      1 ....

      2 ....

         a ....

         b ....

II ....
III ....
    A ....
    B ....

Remember that an outline is more than a mere succession of headings and subheadings. It must indicate the relationship as well as the sequence of parts. It is your opportunity to order and proportion your work while the ideas are still fluid, before some of them have been set down in a form that makes further adjustments laborious and complicated.

The conventional form of outline is characterized by two systematic arrangements: indentation and numbering or lettering. These are meaningful. Coördination of items having approximately the same importance and bearing is indicated by equal indentation and consecutive numbers or letters. Subordination of one topic to another is indicated by deeper indentation and subsequent position of the subordinated topic, and by numbering or lettering in a different series.

Coördination
    1. City government
    2. State government

Subordination
    1. City government
        a. The mayor
        b. The council[1]

The relationship between 1 and 2 is a relationship of coördination; but *a* is subordinate to 1.

The Relationship between Coördinate Headings. Logically, the proper connective (implied if not expressed) between two coördinate headings is *and,* or any word that means pure addition.

---

1 If only one subheading occurs to you for a topic, try to incorporate it in the wording of the topic itself. For example, write:
    II. Large, sparsely populated states like Montana are hard for salesmen to cover.
Do not spread it out like this:
    II. Large, sparsely populated states are hard for salesmen to cover.
        A. Montana.

Headings which are not related to each other by simple addition should not be coördinated. They should either be altered to bring about the required mutual relationship, or some of them should be subordinated to others, depending upon their inter-relationships and relative importance.

The Relationship between a Subordinate Heading and the Heading to Which It Is Subordinated is less uniform. Three connectives (each has equivalents) cover most common·cases. They are: *that is* (when the subheadings analyze the main heading into parts which, taken together, make up the whole)[1]; *for example* (when the subheadings illustrate or give analogies, but do not, together, add up to the heading which precedes them) ;[2] *for* (when the subheadings argue for the truth of the preceding statement).[3] Subheadings which are subordinate to the same heading should be coördinate with each other and, like all coördinates, should be expressed in identical form. Thus a phrase should be coördinated with similar phrases. Modifiers should go with other modifiers of the same expression.[4] Relationships that could be expressed by *but* or *though* are generally misleading or illogical between parts of an outline; in most such cases the thought in the material does not quite square with the meaning of the outline form, for the subheadings tend to disprove the main heading, which is nevertheless

---

1 Example: Three means of instruction are used: (*that is*),
    1. Textbook
    2. Lecture
    3. Recitation

2 Example: Some good novels are not well received at first. (*For example*),
    1. *Henry Esmond* was refused by several publishers.
    2. *Maurice Guest* was little known for many years.

3 Example: The typewriter should have a standard keyboard: (*for*),
    1. It promotes speed and accuracy.
    2. Others besides the owner can use it readily.
    3. It brings a better price for re-sale or turn-in.

4 Some lists of good coördinates:

men	too soft
money	broken at the top
ammunition	small and shrunken
(all nouns)	(all adjective modifiers of the same idea)

        The goods are damaged.
        The charge is excessive.
        (both complete statements)

87

stated as being true. This way of reasoning, if not downright illogical, is a short cut that had better be expanded.[1]

The Sentence Outline. A topic outline, expressed merely in words and phrases, does well enough in a first draft, while the general plan for the composition is taking form. But before beginning to write your essay, you should make a sentence outline. This should begin with your thesis. Each main heading of the outline should grow out of the thesis and point directly to the conclusion (the substance of the independent clause in the thesis). A sentence outline is made of complete sentences. Each heading or subheading may be a sentence in itself.

I. The Democrats cannot win this election.
    A. They have a weak candidate.
    B. The liberal Republican candidate has attracted many Democratic voters.

Or sentences may be run over from part to part.

I. The movement has two causes:
    A. Depression,
    B. Irresponsible leadership;
II. And three results:
    A. Growing class consciousness,
    B. Loss of local self-reliance,
    C. New confidence among the poor, because of their recent successes.

In this latter arrangement no heading is used which is not either a sentence in itself or a part of some sentence that is completed in the outline. The advantage of a sentence outline is its scrupulous

---

1 A misleading short cut:
  A. The resort is popular, but
    1. The mornings are foggy;
    2. There are many mosquitoes;
    3. Accommodations are inadequate.
An expanded form in which the reasoning is complete and logical:
  A. The resort has several drawbacks: for example,
    1. The mornings are foggy;
    2. There are many mosquitoes;
    3. Accommodations are inadequate.
  B. It has many advantages, however, which keep it popular: for example,
    1. The fishing is excellent;
    2. The food is unexcelled;
    3. The nights are cool;
    4. The same congenial guests return every summer.

explicitness. It indicates not only what is to be treated, but, to an extent, just what is to be said about it. It leaves fewer vaguenesses that may mean trouble later.

Before you begin to write any part of your essay, make the sentence outline a test of your proposed structure. Be sure that every section of the work has adequate substantiation. Be especially careful that the various parts have their justification in the conclusion (are not mere padding), and that the conclusion is the logical outcome of the preceding material (not just something tacked on). An outline so used is an excellent help in the arduous, important task of competent thinking on an extensive scale.

An Outline Showing All Three Processes of Development. In the following outline, heading I is developed by analysis, II by illustration, III by argument. In I, notice that, since the process is analysis, A + B + C = I. Notice that the connective *and* is appropriate in the outline as follows: I *and* II *and* III; A *and* B *and* C; 1 *and* 2 *and* 3, etc. For clarity in this outline, the connectives between heads and their subheads are explicitly stated. Notice that in II and III the connective applies to *each* of the subheads concerned, not just to the first. Thus: *for example,* A; *for example,* B; *for example,* C. This may seem a very elementary observation, but it is often unhappily forgotten by makers of outlines.

BOETHIUS TO-DAY

Thesis. Though the appeal of Boethius to-day is different from the appeal which made his name a power in the Middle Ages, he clarifies that period for us better than Augustine does.

I.   Three reasons account for the overwhelming influence of Boethius upon the Middle Ages. *That is:*

A.   His works were the channel through which they received a large proportion of what they got from classical antiquity.

B.   He was considered a Christian martyr.

C.   His *Consolation of Philosophy* was a phenomenally popular book.

II.   The study of Boethius affords much that is of modern interest: *for example,*

    A.   An outstanding political career in trying times;

    B.   Notable achievements in many fields, *for example,*

        1.   Invention,

        2.   Mathematics,

        3.   Music,

        4.   Religion,

        5.   Philosophy,

        6.   Literature;

    C.   Several unsolved problems, *for example,*

        1.   In what sense was he a Christian?

        2.   Was he involved in a plot against Theodoric?

III.   To many a modern student Boethius clarifies the interests of the Middle Ages more fully than does Augustine, *for:*

    A.   His writings deal more systematically with non-religious medieval interests.

    B.   His medieval influence upon the educational system persists in some ways even to-day.

CHAPTER SEVEN

Writing and Documenting the Paper

Write your paper and provide necessary footnotes, following the suggestions in this chapter.[1]

For illustrations of matters discussed in this chapter, see the specimen essay, pp. 103-157.

WRITING

Special Problems in Writing a Research Paper. The writing of a research paper, once the outline is made, involves a few problems not so likely to come up in other kinds of composition. To what extent and how should the author show his own personality in the essay? How can the necessary borrowed and quoted materials be harmonized into a unity of effect? How can so large and complicated a study be made clear and interesting?

The Author's Personality. You can hardly forget that the essay is not about you, but about your study. You are right in not entering the picture yourself any more than is necessary. The story of how you first thought of writing on this subject, for example, should probably be dispensed with. At some points, perhaps, if a personal matter has real value, it may be included in a footnote. But do not feel, on the other hand, that you have to efface yourself entirely. Referring to yourself as "we," "one," or "a mere beginner in this field" is likely to seem awkward. Don't be afraid to say "I" when that is what you mean. "I am convinced" is less presumptuous than "everyone agrees," and probably more accurate. "I have not found" is generally better than "no one has ever discovered." But above all, do not let the desirableness of decorum

---

1 You should document the paper with most of the requisite footnotes as you write. But for the purpose of clarity in explaining, the two processes are treated separately in this chapter.

and correctness lead you to think that research requires either a depersonalized or a grand manner of writing. Your language may be as brilliant, original, and interesting as you can make it, so long as it keeps correctness, relevance, and an appropriate but not too stiff dignity.

Dominating and Assimilating Borrowed Materials. You are not merely compiling facts and quotations. No matter how extensive and complicated your materials, one test of your adequacy as a writer is the extent to which you can turn out a work in a prevailing style of its own. Therefore your direct quotations must not be so long or so numerous as to seem to take the essay quite out of your own hands, and give it a confusion of styles. Unless there is some clear advantage in quotation, put as many of the ideas as possible into your own words. When another writer's language is needed try to quote directly only such phrases as give the passage appropriate distinction. Longer quotations, when advantageous, may of course be used. You should be able to judge for yourself about how much quoted matter your essay will carry without losing its own individual style.

Paraphrases and indirect quotations should not be put in quotation marks, though the source of the material should be acknowledged in a footnote.

Short direct quotations, in quotation marks, should be continuous with your text, and not separately paragraphed like dialogue in a story. Example (asterisks show points needing source footnotes):

> The Confederates advanced in their characteristic "open style," for they placed great faith in the colonel's word that "raw troops can never execute a successful ambuscade."* One diary even mentions that they hummed a hymn tune as they crossed the bridge.*

In a typewritten manuscript, long quotations may be "displayed." That is, you may single-space them and set them in from the margin on each side. With such an arrangement, quotation marks are not used.

Readability and Interest. Any attractiveness in your writing should grow out of your personal feeling for the task. This feeling, concern, or conviction must be sincere, for purely decorative or sprightly language artificially inserted will only seem out of place in a research paper. And the effect of even your sincere feeling must be controlled so as not to impair the desirable spirit of objectivity. Yet the mere existence of your interest is not enough. It must evidence itself in the language you use. Stress vigor and economy of expression, concreteness, directness, the right amount of emphasis where emphasis belongs. Avoid extravagance, pretentiousness, wordiness, pointless repetition, ambiguity, plodding literalness. For your illustrations, select material that has character and, if possible, some narrative interest. In presenting the body of your work, do not slight the dramatic, the colorful, the distinctive. Such appeals, when they do not warp and misrepresent your materials, are legitimate aids in promoting that vitality which every writer desires to achieve in an article. There is no reason, therefore, why a solid, responsible piece of writing should not be interesting and readable.

DOCUMENTATION WITH FOOTNOTES

Purposes of Footnotes. Footnotes convey matters, such as sources, that would interrupt the continuity of your text. But why include such matters at all? Why not avoid them, as popular essayists do, if the information concerned is so distantly relevant as to seem an interruption? In a word, footnotes are used for helpfulness. You assume that your reader is reading for more than amusement. He really wants to master your subject. Therefore, if you have suggestive backgrounds of thought or fact, beyond your immediate purpose, you may well offer that further help in a footnote. The footnote form will indicate secondary relevance to the main argument, but the information will still be available to those interested. Thus may be included comparisons interesting mostly to those familiar with similar studies; queries that may be suggestive and fruitful to some readers, but of which you do not see any clear issue; criticisms that should be mentioned for the sake of completeness, though you doubt if they have much value or force; and information that more fully places and identifies your materials, but does not promote their part in your particular study. Sometimes if you feel that further information would be out of place in your work, your footnote may call attention to sources where the matter is extensively treated. The commonest type of footnote refers to the source of facts or quoted words. Such notes may serve any of the following purposes. (a) They may make it legal to publish substance or words from another writer. Such publication unacknowledged might justify a suit for plagiarism. (b) They carry out an old tradition of honor among scholars, a tradition which requires the acknowledgment of credit where it is due. (c) They enable a reader independently to consult sources of information. (d) In the coöperative world of modern scholarship, they furnish other scholars full information regarding sources; so that such scholars may relate the study to their own researches, or themselves contribute to the problem with which the article deals.

Footnotes are not for ostentatious display of learning. They are not a meaningless convention or fashion. They should not be used when they are not needed. No footnote, for example, need explain the source of facts that are commonly known or that have only an incidental relation to the study. You will not be challenged, for instance, if you happen to observe, without citing your authority, that the earth is spherical. Very familiar quotations, if they are used not as subjects of study or definite means of research, but only as part of the general language of the essay, may also appear without notation of their source. Thus you may write that the quality of mercy is not strained or that the proper study of mankind is man, even without quotation marks, for no one will suspect you of trying to steal expressions which have become common property for all users of the language. Therefore, if you feel that the triteness of such quotations does not, in a certain passage, impair your style, you are welcome to them.

When to Use a Footnote. (a) A footnote is needed to give the source of any fact that is so recently or so little known as not to be common property. If you are in doubt regarding the familiarity of a fact, be on the safe side and annotate. When several facts in a passage are drawn from the same source, one footnote at the end of the passage may serve for all. (b) A direct quotation that is not common property should be followed by a footnote giving the exact source. (c) Any plan or organization of material, such as an arrangement of statistics, should be ascribed to its source. (d) Whenever you express a sentiment, theory, or opinion derived from another writer, though you agree, you should acknowledge the source. And you should be careful not to ascribe to the other writer any incidental attitude which is only your own, not his, or to claim credit for anything that is his. This calls for clarity of understanding and expression. (e) Besides these obligatory footnotes, you may put into explanatory notes any incidental matter that you consider not sufficiently relevant to go in the text and yet too important to be left out altogether.

How to Put a Footnote into Your Essay. Some books put all notes at the end of the volume. Generally printers prefer to have footnotes inserted in the manuscript immediately after the passage which they annotate. In some works a system of asterisks and daggers indicates the notes; in some a series of index numbers begins anew on each page. Each system is designed to serve its particular purpose. The following arrangement which is required in your paper is a convenient one very commonly used.

Just after the passage to be annotated place a number, raised a little above the line. Number the first footnote 1 and the others in a continuous series to the end of the essay. Do not begin a new series on each page.

> Example: The opposing forces included some 8570 men who had enlisted early,[1] and a small number of recent recruits from neighboring villages.[2]

Saving enough space at the bottom of the page for footnotes that are to be entered there, draw a line from margin to margin beneath your text.

Below the line enter the footnotes for that page, in order, single-spaced. Precede each note by its appropriate number.

Kinds of Footnotes.

Source Notes. Just what material goes into a source footnote depends partly upon what information has been given in the text, and partly upon whether or not the paper includes a separate bibliographical list. Since economy and avoidance of repetition are desirable, a footnote should not ordinarily repeat an author's name or a title which has been adequately stated in the text. If there is a separate bibliographical list (and your paper will have one), the footnote may leave out such details as place, publisher, and date of a book. If a separate bibliographical list were not given, the publisher and place of publication would be optional in footnotes, but the date of any work should be given in the first footnote citing that work. The source note should be exact, referring to a page in a particular edition; to act, scene, and lines in poetic plays; to line numbers in poems that have numbered lines. For very famous works the author's last name is often enough, without initials or first name. Example: Milton's *Paradise Lost,* Book 4, 1. 27.

The form for bibliographical references in footnotes is much the same, except for matter omitted, as it is in bibliographies. But since footnotes are not alphabetized, the author's last name should not be written first. As for punctuation, the author's name, and the title of the work are followed by commas, rather than by periods.

When one of your source notes has once cited a book or article, you may use the following devices to avoid repeating the full reference over and over.

Ibid. (Latin, *ibidem,* in the same place.) This abbreviation, used instead of an author's name and a title, means that the reference is to the same work cited immediately before. If there are intervening references to other books, the device is not to be used.

Example:

14. Fyodor Dostoevski, *The Possessed,* pp. 145-178.
15. Ibid.
16. Ibid., p. 156.

In this example, footnote 15 refers to the same pages mentioned in the preceding note.

Op. cit. or Loc. cit. (Latin, *opere citato,* or *loco citato,* in the work or place cited.) This abbreviation, after the author's name, means that the reference is to a work or passage by this author, which has been cited in an earlier footnote. If the author concerned has been cited for more than one book, the abbreviation will not serve.

To refer to preceding or following pages of your own essay, write *See above, p. 9,* or *See below, p. 17.*

There are many other permissible footnote abbreviations, most of them less important or less common. Many of them are in Latin. Footnote abbreviations, when notes are plentiful, save considerable space and expense in printing. Most of them are conventional, and quite familiar to users of technical writings. But do not imagine that any value comes from the mere employment of such learned jargon. Save for a few simple abbreviations like the following, you can do very well with plain English written out in full.

Art. Article.

c. (Latin, *circa,* about. Sometimes abbreviated to *ca.*) Approximately. Generally with a date.

cf. (Latin, *confer,* compare.)

chap., *plural,* chaps. Chapter.

col., *plural,* cols. Column.

ed., *plural,* eds. Edited, editor, edition.

et al. And others.

et seq. And the following.

infra. Below.

f., *plural,* ff. After a page number, this abbreviation means that the discussion referred to goes on through one or several following pages.

Fig., *plural,* Figs. Figure. Refers to diagrams, graphs, drawings.

l., *plural,* ll. Line.

no., *plural,* nos. Number.

p., plural, pp. Page. Examples: P. 17; pp. 112-139; p. 19 f.; pp. 47 ff.

passim. Here and there. Used when the reference is to something scattering or to a general attitude expressed in various parts of a book.

sic. Thus. Used in brackets within a quotation to show that the preceding expression, no matter how strange or incorrect it may seem, is exactly quoted.

q.v. (Latin, *quod vide,* which see.)

r. (Latin, *recto,* right.)

sec. Section.

Ser. Series.

supra. Above.

tr. Translator, translation.

v. (Latin, *vide,* see; Latin, *verso,* left.)

vol., *plural,* vols. Volume.

Explanatory Notes. Since the material of an explanatory note is less important or less relevant than the text of your article, the note should be worded more briefly. Sometimes referring to sources of full information is better than attempting your own account. But original footnotes are a good place for personal opinions, remarks regarding possible by-products of your study, collateral information, recommendations for further reading, incidental comparisons, or suggestions of related queries and problems. In reading over an early draft, if you find your essay long and not always to the point, you may effect an improvement by relegating some of the material, condensed, to the status of explanatory footnotes.

Chapter Eight

Arrangement of the Bibliography

Assemble and classify the list of works that you have used.
Follow the principles described in this chapter.

See the specimen bibliography, pp. 155-157.

The bibliography cards which you assembled in your first search for material have made a preliminary, working bibliography. Some of the books and articles there listed you may not have used. In writing your paper, you may have added other titles. Now it is time to gather together and arrange the list of works that you did use. There may be five or six; for an extensive study there may be a hundred or more. This selected list is your essay bibliography.

The contents of these cards are to be copied as a helpful list, to support and supplement your paper. In what order should the various titles appear in such a list? The answer to that question depends upon the size of the list, and upon the nature of its contents and functions. Following are some of the commonest arrangements, together with a few of their advantages, uses, and limitations. You should select for your own use the system which best suits your present purpose.

Alphabetical Order. Generally the simplest and best arrangement for a short bibliography is the alphabetical order of the authors' last names. In following this sequence, you should place unsigned items in the alphabetical list by their title. Though such an arrangement has no rime or reason beyond its arbitrary alphabetical order, it has the great advantage of being in itself a kind of index.

Chronological Order. Some lists of books are most convenient if arranged in the chronological order of their publication.

The chronological order is especially appropriate whenever a historical or developmental plan prevails. A long chronological list cannot be used conveniently without an index.

Classification of Items According to Divisions of the Subject. Works on history, for example, might be classified according to countries; works on education might be divided according to the various levels, such as elementary, secondary, and advanced education. This arrangement may be helpful if the study itself follows the same plan, but the classification often involves difficulties when some works cover several of the divisions. A section may be needed for miscellaneous references. A supplementary index may be required if the list is very long.

Classification of Items Based upon Kinds of Works Listed. Writers sometimes desire to make separate divisions for primary sources and secondary sources, for books and periodicals, for signed works and unsigned works. Reference works may form a division by themselves. Such classification is often useful to a writer who wants evidence of a well rounded and representative study. It may prove unhandy to a reader seeking a particular title. Some works also are likely to fall into more than one class, as when a book contains both primary and secondary material. If such a list is long, an index is required.

CHAPTER NINE

Revision

Revise your paper according to the directions in this chapter.

Forget all about the paper for a day or even for a week before you revise it. If you try to make corrections as soon as you have finished the writing, your memory of what you meant to write may be so strong that you will overlook the shortcomings of what you actually wrote.

First go through the essay as a whole, making sure that in every part it clearly conveys the unity, proportion, and logical structure of your outline. Does the introduction clearly state your subject, objective, and method of treatment? Are the main headings given proportionate space and emphasis? Do the transitions indicate progress towards your objective? Is the conclusion, when reached, convincing and clear, leaving the dominant impression that you desire for your essay?

See if you can defend the structure of each paragraph. Would any one of your paragraphs be better as two? Should several paragraphs be combined into one? Do most of your paragraphs not only state an idea, but develop it (by argument, illustration, or analysis)?

Is there a good reason for each punctuation mark used? Is your meaning at any point vague, ambiguous, or misleading for lack of needed punctuation?

Do all your adjectives and adverbs clearly modify the ideas you want them to modify? Do your pronouns clearly refer to their antecedents? Are the various time levels made clear by proper tenses or adverbial modifiers?

101

Are your grammar and spelling correct? When in doubt, consult your dictionary. Do not "take a chance" that you may be right.

Remember that great care and accuracy are needed at every point for good research.

THE FINAL FORM

Copy your work according to the following directions.

Make your final copy from a correct, complete manuscript. Accurate copying is almost impossible when the task is complicated by the necessity of at the same time correcting, amplifying, checking, or skipping about for only partly assembled material.

Have your writing or typewriting readable and uncrowded (double-spaced on the typewriter, or written on paper with well spaced lines), with wide margins. Save plenty of room for the single-spaced footnotes at the bottom of the page. But accuracy is more important than neatness. Never hesitate to make needed corrections, though they may mar the appearance of a page.[1]

---

1 An excellent guide to punctuation is Harry Shaw, *Punctuate It Right!* (New York: Barnes and Noble, Inc., 1963). For detailed information about capitalization, spelling, abbreviations, footnotes, and bibliographies, see *A Manual of Style* (11th ed.; Chicago: University of Chicago Press, 1949). For guides to meaning, pronunciation, and spelling of words, see Harry Shaw, *Errors in English and Ways to Correct Them* (New York: Barnes and Noble, Inc., 1962).

A Specimen Term Paper

The following article is written for the purpose of illustrating the work taught in this book. Therefore all the documents used are such as an undergraduate might find in his college library. All definite citations are referred to their sources in footnotes, in some cases with more liberal preciseness than might be found in a professional research study. And it is hoped that the article, though somewhat longer than you may be required to write, avoids the air of pretentious dullness which is the besetting sin, but not a necessary characteristic, of documented papers. Notice that the exacting requirements of responsible research are here found consistent with some wit, a certain amount of original reflection, and some obvious interest in the subject.

The method used is in the main that of the case study (see page 82)—the detailed, systematic, analytical examination of a limited subject. Some parts of the historical method are used at certain points. The main characteristic of the method as here used is the resolution of a complex phenomenon into its natural elements so as to discover the principle which makes those elements into a unified whole. An examination of the thesis will show how the process works in this particular article. Of course the thesis stands merely as a hypothesis until the study substantiates it. And since this is only a case study, the utmost dependable results will be limited to a more thorough understanding of the subject itself, without reference to relations among other subjects.

THE TRIPLE PERSONALITY OF ALICE
OUTLINE

THESIS. The historical Alice Liddell, the fictional Alice of Wonderland, and the doll-like figure drawn by Tenniel blend in a reader's mind as a complex introverted escapist whose experience with the external adult world leads to a decided preference for imaginative childhood.

INTRODUCTION. The triple personality of Alice is more complex than the dual personality of Lewis Carroll.

I.   The "real" Alice Liddell was a mild, imaginative child.

    A. Photographs show her dreamy-eyed, while her sisters seem alert to the present external situation.

    B. The restraints of their academic Victorian residence developed in all three sisters a deceptive external primness cloaking natural high spirits.

    C. Alice's mild tones, her request for nonsense, and her earnest insistence that the tale of Wonderland be written suggest an unusual absorption in imaginative interests.

II.   The "ideal" Alice, like Lewis Carroll himself, tends to ignore the material, external world, favoring the inner world of imagination.

    A. Realistically presented in most details, she illustrates, practices, and incorporates a deliberate philosophy of dreams as the way of life.

B. She, like Lewis Carroll, shows the weaknesses and advantages of word-mindedness, giving abstract concepts preference over concrete experience.

C. Her evasive, dream quality may be partly due to the author's use of her as a substitute for the normal adult love life which he lacked.

III. Tenniel's drawings lead some readers to overlook the important function of Alice as a bulwark against the stultifications of our adult social world.

A. Tenniel's pictures of Alice miss her complexity and inwardness.

B. Though these drawings may dominate conceptions of Alice retained from a childhood impression, adult rereading of the story corrects the resultant error.

THE TRIPLE PERSONALITY OF ALICE*

George Shelton.Hubbell

Alice Pleasance Liddell was born on May 24, 1852, while her scholarly father was headmaster of Westminster School. In 1855 her father was made Dean of Christ Church College, Oxford, and she came to Oxford at the age of four.[1] There, hardly

---

1. Her father was Henry George Liddell (1811-1898), Dean of Christ Church College for thirty-six years (1855-1891), and famous to students of Greek as co-editor of Liddell and Scott's Greek-English Lexicon (1843). Dean Liddell had four daughters and three sons, but one girl, Rhoda, was too young for the wonderland adventure, and the boys would not have counted anyhow, for Lewis Carroll did not find boys congenial. The best account of Dean Liddell is H. L. Thompson's Memoir of H. G. Liddell, D.D. (1889). Thompson also wrote the article on Liddell for the Dictionary of National Biography. There is a portrait of Dean Liddell in S. D. Collingwood's The Life and Letters of Lewis Carroll, p. 213. At the time of Alice's death in 1934 only three members of her father's family survived: Rhoda, the younger sister, at whose house in Westerham in Kent Alice died; Sir Frederick, legal adviser to the speaker of the House of Commons; and Lionel, living in Dinard on the French coast.

---

* Reprinted, with permission of the editor, from *The Sewanee Review*, vol. 48, pp. 174-96 (April, 1940).

more than a baby, she became the favorite companion
of the young, distinguished professor Charles
Lutwidge Dodgson, an able mathematician not yet
known as Lewis Carroll, and in his mind she finally
precipitated the remarkable tale later to be entitled Alice's Adventures in Wonderland. She
was the "original Alice." There is also, to be
sure, the "ideal Alice" of the story, who, being
a creature of the author's fancy, differs in some
respects from the actual child. And finally there
is, for many readers, a third Alice, whom Sir John
Tenniel drew, the likeness of another little girl,
for his famous illustrations.[2] Can we form a
rationale of these three Alices, explain them,
harmonize them? Some writers have made much of
the dual personality which enabled the Reverend

---

2. His model was not Alice Liddell, but a younger
girl named Mary Hilton Badcock. See Williams and
Madan, A Handbook of the Literature of the Rev.
C. L. Dodgson, p. 22, for a portrait and account of
Mary Badcock. She was daughter of Canon Badcock
of Ripon. Smaller than Alice Liddell and less
piquant, she had "bright golden hair" combed
straight back in the manner made familiar by the
Tenniel drawings. Dodgson was struck by seeing
her photograph, and recommended her to Tenniel as
a model. The artist visited her, but worked largely from photographs. He did not like to draw
from models.

Professor Dodgson, normally a severe scholar, to
assume the role of Lewis Carroll, sprightly friend
of little girls. The triple personality of his
Alice, as it comes complexly to a reader, is also
of great interest.

I

First we must look carefully at the "real
Alice," for she it was whom Lewis Carroll set out
to portray, and his literary replica of her is in
many respects not unrealistic. Alice Liddell was
ten in 1862, when the story of her "adventures" was
conceived as a book. She lived in the northeast
angle of "Tom Quad," and her professorial chum
lived in the northwest angle. She and her two
sisters always wore cotton dresses, just alike and
quite as full as the dresses in the Tenniel illustrations.[3] Her dark hair was bobbed so as to
come a little below her ears, and she wore bangs
like many little girls of to-day. That she was
pretty and graceful many of Lewis Carroll's camera

---

3.   Yet Lewis Carroll wrote to Tenniel, "Don't
give Alice so much crinoline." Stuart Collingwood, op. cit., p. 130.

studies of her attest. Belle Moses has vividly
described some of those photographs.

"One, as a beggar child, has become quite
famous. She is pictured standing, with her
ragged dress slipping from her shoulders and
her right hand held as if begging for pennies; the
other hand rests upon her hip, and her head is
bent in a meek fashion: but the mouth has a
roguish curve, and there is just the shadow of
a laugh in the dark eyes, for of course it's
only 'make believe,' and no one knows it better
than Alice herself."[4]

All three of the sisters were pretty. Alice
was the middle one, and in some respects the
others were both prettier than she, but she had a
lively charm and an imaginative expression that
may account for Lewis Carroll's preference. Miss
Moses remarks this in a group portrait of the
three.

---

4. Belle Moses, Lewis Carroll in Wonderland
and at Home, p. 87. Lewis Carroll, who liked
child actors, often posed the children so as to
suggest a fictitious situation or story. This
picture is reproduced in Collingwood, op. cit.,
p. 80.

"He took another picture of the children perched upon a sofa: Lorina in the center, a little sister nestling close to her on either side, making a pretty pyramid of the three dark heads. Yet in studying the faces one can understand why it was Alice who inspired him . . . Alice, with the elflocks and the straight heavy 'bang,' is looking far away with those wonderful eyes of hers . . . If it hadn't been for Alice there would have been no Wonderland."[5] And Alice's pensive, far-away look in this picture may well indicate that her thoughts were indeed in Wonderland, for we learn that Lewis Carroll generally told the children stories to put them in the mood for having portraits taken.[6]

In a third picture, elaborately posed by their gifted friend, Alice is seated on a table, probably in his study.[7] She holds a bunch of

---

5. Moses, op. cit., pp. 87-88. The picture is in Collingwood, op. cit., p. 94.
6. Caryl Hargreaves, "Lewis Carroll As Recalled by Alice," New York Times, May 1, 1932, sec. 6, p. 7. Caryl Hargreaves is the son of Alice.
7. There is a photograph of this famous study in Collingwood, op. cit., p. 134.

dark grapes on a dish in her lap. Lorina stands back to her, holding a few grapes just above the reach of Edith, who seems trying to get them. Lorina and Edith really appear interested in the little affair of the grapes, but Alice has a rapt, inner look which may be a result of the recent story. All three wear voluminous white striped frocks which make their goodly childish legs seem puny, unlike the perhaps too mature rounding of Alice's legs in the Tenniel drawings. And though Alice shows something of the Tenniel grace, in the photograph it seems more natural, not so suggestive of dancing school.[8]

Such was the child for whom and about whom the Alice books were written. In 1862, at the age of ten, and looking probably very much as she appears in these portraits, she went on a customary boat trip up the Thames from Oxford to Godstow with her two sisters, Professor Dodgson, and a certain friendly Professor Duckworth. On that

---

8. This picture is reproduced in the New York Times, May 1, 1932, sec. 5, p. 7.

trip Dodgson so moved her with his tales and
jingles that she drew from him the rash promise
to write the book of <u>Alice's</u> <u>Adventures</u> <u>Under-
ground,</u> as he called it then. One account of
the trip is preserved in the well-known pref-
atory poem beginning, "All in the golden
afternoon." There Lorina is represented as Prima,
Alice as Secunda, and Edith as Tertia. Secunda,
or Alice, it is significant to note, was the
one who asked for nonsense in the story. The
tale had come out painfully, subject to interruptions by Tertia "not <u>more</u> than once a minute."
Episodes had been produced on former trips. Verses
and drawings had been added in the professor's
study, in the boat, beneath a hayrick in a field.
Sometimes, Alice wrote afterwards, "Mr. Dodgson, in the middle of the telling of a thrilling
adventure, would pretend to go fast asleep, to
our great dismay."[9] But after that particular

9. Quoted in Collingwood, op. cit., p. 96.
Apparently these river trips were frequent, habitual summer occurrences. At these times, Lewis
Carroll always relaxed from his customary dignity
by wearing white flannel trousers and a hard

trip of July 4, Alice most persistently teased
her friend later in his rooms, till he agreed to
write the stories down, as he recorded for the
day in his journal.[10] "I wonder how many stories
the world has missed," she reflected long afterwards, "because he never wrote anything down
till I teased him into doing it."[11] And Lewis
Carroll himself confided to her in 1883, when she
was a grown woman, that without her "infant
patronage I might never have written at all."[12]

---

straw hat. As for the figure cut by Alice herself, one gets a lively idea of it in the passage
about Alice rowing with the sheep in Through the
Looking-Glass. It was Professor Dodgson who
taught the real Alice how to row. The same five
usually went along. Once, Alice recalled later,
two of Dodgson's sisters (then in their twen-
ties) went with them, somewhat awing the children,
precluding the customary stories and tea. The
tea was a definite attraction for the Liddells,
who had no afternoon refreshments at home at
that period. This fact may have suggested the
idea of the mad tea party. It may be significant
that "Beautiful Soup" was Alice's favorite of
the poems. Alice was not the only one of the
group to get into the story as a character. Lorina
was the Lory, Edith the Eaglet, Professor Duckworth the Duck, and Dodgson the Dodo. See Caryl
Hargreaves, op. cit., p. 7.

10. See Collingwood, op. cit., p. 94.
11. Quoted in The Literary Digest, vol. 113,
May 21, 1932, p. 16.
12. Quoted by Caryl Hargreaves, op. cit., p. 15.

One can hardly overrate the importance of Alice Liddell in the making of the books named for her. It is not simply that the heroine is Lewis Carroll's conscientious representation of her, bearing her name. Her part in the work is still more fundamental. He considered eight or nine possible titles for the story, but each one began with <u>Alice</u>.[13] She, it seems, was the one indispensable element there. When the

---

13. In his customary methodical way, he arranged these suggested titles and gave his objections to some of them, about as follows:

Alice's Adventures under Ground
("About mines?")
Alice's Golden House
("Already a book called Lily's Golden Hours.")

Alice among the {Elves / Goblins

Alice's {Hour / Doings / Adventures} in {Elf-land / Wonderland}

What excellent taste he manifested in his final choice! That the word "golden" was a special weakness of his may be seen in two of the Alice poems: "All in the golden afternoon" (p. 13); "Lingering in the golden gleam" (p. 272). In the introductory poem to <u>Sylvie</u> <u>and</u> <u>Bruno</u> occurs: "Seen faintly in the golden gleam" (p. 275). <u>The</u> <u>Hunting</u> <u>of</u> <u>the</u> <u>Snark</u> is inscribed to Gertrude Chataway "in memory of golden summer hours" (p. 756).

book was finally printed, July 4, 1865, just three years after the memorable trip up the river, Alice received the first impression, Princess Beatrice the second.[14] In the later story <u>Through</u> <u>the</u> <u>Looking-Glass,</u>[15] the initial letters of the lines that make up the concluding poem, when read downward, spell her full name -- Alice Pleasance Liddell. What sort of girl was she?

It has been suggested that she was prim. G. K. Chesterton thought that Lewis Carroll's imaginary Alice was probably "much more imaginable than the real one. Both perhaps exhibited the primness of their period: in both perhaps the primness was more formal than real."[16] Certainly the Victorian training of Alice was sufficiently stiff and illiberal. Her son has recorded that she and her sisters were never allowed to go for walks with other children.

---

14. Collingwood, op. cit., p. 104.
15. P. 272.
16. "The 100th Birthday of Nonsense," New York <u>Times,</u> Jan. 24, 1932, sec. 2, pp. 1-2, 22.

Their governess, Miss Prickett, not very well
educated or trained for her work, accompanied
them about and gave them all the formal instruction they had. They were not allowed to run or
make any noise near the college. Probably the
jumbled hodge-podge of "manners" and unreliable
information with which Lewis Carroll endows
his imaginary heroine in not uncharacteristic of
the little girl to whom he told the story.[17]

But certainly "the cruel three" of the boat
trips, among congenial friends, away from the
restraints of an adultish university, showed
little sign of manners or primness. The imperious edict to begin the story, the rude and frequent interruptions, the alert and saucy quip
that "it _is_ next time,"[18] seem believable and
humanly childish enough to satisfy Mr. Chesterton, or any one. Indeed this passage and Alice's
persistent and successful campaign of teasing
for the written story, suggest that Lewis

---

17. See Caryl Hargreaves, op. cit., p. 7.
18. _Wonderland_, p. 14.

Carroll knew whereof he spoke when he said that his heroine was "always ready for a little argument."[19]

On the other hand, Alice Liddell seems to have been an imaginative, thoughtful, affectionate little girl. Invariable indications of this appear in the pictures which Lewis Carroll took of the three sisters. Secunda, it will be remembered, spoke "in gentler tones."[20] That she responded to the affection of her kind friend with more than a mere childish thirst for stories may be indicated by the fact that she never forgot his failure to call upon her while she lay for six weeks with a broken leg.[21] She was ap-

_____

19. Looking-Glass, p. 250.
20. Wonderland, p. 13.
21. In fact, though he sent many letters (now lost) to the children at the deanery, he seldom came there. See Caryl Hargreaves, op. cit., p. 7. There may have been some tension between him and their father. Dodgson was loyal to Dean Liddell through several conspicuous academic rows which troubled that executive's long and turbulent regime, but the younger man often showed a liberal tendency to side with the students. See Williams and Madan, op. cit., p. xiii. It is probable also that he cared little for parents as a class, particularly for male

parently fond of animals, especially of her cat
Dinah, which the librarian at the college recol-
lects having often chased from the library.[22]
It is interesting that the Cheshire Cat was her
favorite character in the Alice books.[23]   In
fact, the little we know or can infer regarding
her character seems to accord with Adler's
theory of the in-between child in a family, while
Lorina's imperious, edict-giving tendency and
Edith's irresponsible interruptions fit the same
general family pattern.[24]

---

parents. Since his freedom to associate with the
children depended upon parental consent, he
naturally could not very well express such a
feeling, but the icy silence or dry brevity regarding parents in all his letters to children seems significant. In one of his prefaces
he criticizes the parental management of children in church. See Williams and Madan, op.
cit., p. 217. In his many contacts with children
he seems always to have propitiated the parents
by meticulous politeness, but he rigidly excluded them from the fun. Doubtless he felt the
need of removing those barriers which ordinary
adults impose between the generations.
22.   Letter to the New York Times, May 8, 1932,
sec. 3, p. 2, col. 4, by Francis Burke Brandt.
23.   New York Times, Ap. 29, 1932, p. 19, col. 7.
24.   See Alfred Adler, The Education of Children,
pp. 137 - 164. For Alice's subsequent life,
see Appendix, p. 49.

II

When we turn from the "real Alice" of the
story to the "ideal Alice," we notice immediately several conspicuous but superficial dif-
ferences.   (1) To begin with, there was her age.
The imaginary Alice is seven in the first tale.
Through the Looking-Glass finds her seven and a
half, for that story is supposed to occur in
the following winter, with an indoor setting in
contrast with the sunny afternoon in the open
which had introduced her to the rabbit hole.
Of course Alice Liddell was ten when the stories
began to be set down in writing, and when
Through the Looking-Glass was published, she
was nineteen, but she had probably been about
seven when the stories were first told.
Though Carroll preferred seven as her
age for purposes of the book, one can't help
suspecting that the account he gives of her
mental and emotional states is really taken from
the ten-year-old level. She seems a little
precocious for seven.   (2) Another difference

is her hair, which the pictures, including those
that Lewis Carroll himself drew for Alice's
Adventures Underground, all represent as longer
than that of Alice Liddell, and not worn with
bangs, but combed straight back.[25] Carroll's
own drawings gave her a part in the middle, such

---

25. I can't explain why Lewis Carroll made this
change. Were the bangs harder for him to draw?
Did he disapprove his favorite's hair-do? Did
he feel that it would be regarded with disfavor
by others? Did he think that a "child of the
pure unclouded brow" should not have the brow
hidden beneath a fringe of straight hair?
Did Alice herself suggest the change? It may
be worth noting that, though Tenniel's drawings
invariably show Alice's hair in good order,
the text remarks that she often gave a "queer little
toss of her head to keep back the wandering hair
that would always get into her eyes" (Wonderland, p. 130. In the Looking-Glass illustrations she has a comb to preserve an even more
exact coiffure (Mary Badcock, Tenniel's child
model, wore such a comb, as shown in the portrait published in Williams and Madan, op.
cit., p. 22), but the text makes the Tiger-lily
complain that her petals do not curl up more
(Looking-Glass, p. 158). The Hatter, with
professional eye, remarks that her hair wanted
cutting (Wonderland, p. 75). It is possible
that this matter of the straight, unruly hair
was a sore point with Alice Liddell, who had two
sisters with curls; and even the "ideal Alice"
seems to have envied one Ada her ringlets
(Wonderland, p. 29). Such feelings may have
contributed to her somewhat introvert habit of
reverie and her tendency to self-distrust.

as may be seen in his photographs of Lorina's curls,[26] but Tenniel drew the straight hair without any part. (3) It is noteworthy also that Lorina and Edith are excluded from the story, save in their minor roles as the Lory and the Eaglet, while the imaginary Alice is supplied with a new, rather vague family. Why is this? Three heroines would probably have been easier to manage than one. Alice, with two companions, would not have been obliged to talk so much to herself. And though they would not all have dreamed the same dream, they could all have been in Alice's dream. Of course the others would have enjoyed being included. But Lewis Carroll apparently wanted Alice alone. It was she, not the others, who had stirred his imagination. For her also he wrote out the story. Unscrupulously he picked his favorite, as no shrewd parent or teacher would dare to do. It is only bachelors, and similar unattached, non-responsible people who may do that with chil-

---

26. Collingwood, op. cit., pp. 94, 358.

dren. Carroll did it regularly, excluding boys, excluding adults, excluding or omitting various children according to their appeal for him. Then too, Alice herself, an introvert in an ever-present family, probably wished to be alone in the dream with the creatures she met there, though she does, in the first unfamiliar experience of that loneliness, "wish they _would_ put their heads down. I am so _very_ tired of being all alone here."[27] However, she soon got over the worst of such feelings and learned self-reliance as she came to understand her own resources and the emptiness of the imposing bluff in the strange beings whom she met. Also, it is likely that Lewis Carroll wished to have her alone in this world he had made for her. Though he would not have admitted it, perhaps, even to himself, he was probably irked with the necessity of including the other children and the faithful Duckworth on all the excursions with

27. _Wonderland,_ p. 30.

Alice. To a considerable extent, they were the liabilities of his delightful outings, bringing necessary but regrettable irrelevancies, imperious, peremptory, intrusive. As for the absent, vague family of the ideal Alice, the parents were coldly, firmly excluded, according to the method ordinarily adopted by Lewis Carroll with real parents in his letters to their children. Though implied in her dream, these fictitious parents were not seen or heard or thought of. One gathers that he agreed with Samuel Butler in wishing fathers and mothers could pass out of the picture as soon as their children were born. The imaginary sister, who does appear in the story, is considerably older than Alice. This seniority enables her to be less competitive and bossy than the actual Lorina, less adultishly remote than a mother. Lewis Carroll uses her to give a sympathetic view of Alice herself, with the "bright eager eyes" and "the little toss of her head," something that the conditions of the story severely excluded elsewhere.[28] Perhaps it is just as well that there could not be more of this kind of thing. The sister also served, but not particularly well, to give a summary recapitulation of Alice's first dream. The hint in Through the Looking-Glass that the sister was more literal, less imaginative than Alice may have been suggested by a characteristic of Lorina.[29] The one other member of this imaginary family to be mentioned is a brother, said to have a Latin grammar. It was probably the grammar that dragged this boy into the story at all. Only in Sylvie and Bruno did Lewis Carroll deign

---

28. Wonderland, p. 130. The conditions of the story should have excluded such references as those to the "little sleeves," "little arms," and, again, "bright eager eyes" in the well-known rowing scene with the sheep (Looking-Glass, p. 204), but when one remembers that this breach of good technique probably indicates the author's powerful memory of just such an episode, in which he himself had the position of the sheep, one loses any inclination to cavil.

29. Looking-Glass, p. 145. The contrast between quick imagination and plodding literalness is a characteristic device for Lewis Carroll's humor. Probably many who thought that as a professor he was dry and humorlessly literal may simply have failed to catch the humor behind his expressions.

to make full recognition that boys exist, by giving one a real part to play.

But aside from these rather unimportant dif-
ferences, the imaginary Alice seems the result of
a careful attempt to create a faithful replica
of the original. Probably such realistic objectivity does more than anything else to distinguish this heroine beyond the other thousands
of child characters in literature. For the
author was not content to give a superficial,
external, or passive likeness of his beloved
young friend. He explored her mind, her temperament, her faults, her idiosyncrasies, with
the probing thoroughness of a lover to whom
every detail is precious; and he gave her in
action. True, as a thoroughgoing Victorian, he
refrained from any of the countless subjects
unmentionable among children of the most genteel
contemporary families. That is a very considerable reservation, and some day it may date
the stories more damagingly than it does now;
but as yet we have not, so far as children's

125

books are concerned, appreciably relinquished

the Victorian reticences. Perhaps this conserva-

tive trait has made books for children seem

more childish to-day than they used to seem, in

the days when books for adults were almost equally

squeamish.

In as far as realism concerns the external

details of life, we learn a great deal about this

imaginary Alice. In her pocket (duly shown in

some of the illustrations[30]) she carried comfits,

a thimble,[31] and, later on, a memorandum book.[32]

She sometimes made daisy chains,[33] played cro-

quet,[34] or chess.[35] She was sometimes punished

for faults which she acknowledged having com-

mitted.[36] She knew how to row, but frequently

---

30. See Wonderland, p. 21. Lewis Carroll's own
pockets must have served much of the time as a
kind of supplement for those of the little girls
he knew or might happen to meet. See Collingwood, op. cit., pp. 369 ff.
31. Wonderland, p. 38.
32. Looking-Glass, p. 213.
33. Wonderland, p. 17.
34. Ibid., p. 89.
35. Looking-Glass, pp. 144-146. Apparently
she liked to play chess.
36. Ibid., p. 198.

"caught crabs."[37] There was an old nurse who ca.
her when it was time to take a walk:[38] and this
nurse she had once frightened by pretending
"that I'm a hungry hyaena, and you're a bone."[39]
She had a governess for lessons,[40] which came at
nine a.m. At one-thirty p.m. she generally
had dinner.[41] She apparently liked orange mar-
malade,[42] but in general didn't care for jam,
at any rate, not to-day.[43] She had at one time
attended a day-school where French and music were
extras.[44] She was thoroughly familiar with
the use of slates.[45]

Such were her important little tastes, experiences, habits: the stuff of which child
character, adult character, and world destiny
are made. Also regarding her temperament and

---

37. Ibid., p. 203. See illustration, p. 206.
38. Wonderland, p. 43.
39. Looking-Glass, p. 145.
40. Ibid., p. 175.
41. Wonderland, p. 78.
42. Wonderland, p. 18.
43. Looking-Glass, pp. 196-197.
44. Wonderland, p. 103.
45. Wonderland, p. 115.

...uch is told. "I wish I could

you half the things Alice used to say, be-

ginning with her favourite phrase 'Let's pre-

tend.' "[46] She often talked to herself, even

scolded herself to tears, tried to box her own

ears, pretended to be two people, and cheated

herself at croquet;[47] or she talked to her

kittens,[48] even contemplated a conversation with

her own feet.[49] In short, she was imaginative,

"a very thoughtful little girl,"[50] a dreamer who

had a certain faith in her dreams, a faith which

Lewis Carroll is willing to encourage on philo-

sophic grounds. "Life, what is it but a dream?"[51]

The question as to whether Alice or the Red

King did the dreaming[52] is especially philosophic,

suggesting that this "ideal Alice" is only a

dream in the mind of the author, and, more re-

---

46. <u>Looking-Glass,</u> pp. 145.
47. <u>Wonderland,</u> pp. 24, 27.
48. <u>Looking-Glass,</u> p. 143.
49. <u>Wonderland,</u> pp. 26-27.
50. <u>Looking-Glass,</u> p. 188.
51. Ibid., p. 272.
52. Ibid., pp. 188-189; 271.

motely still, that we are all dreams in the mind of God. With all her fondness for dreams, Alice did not like the idea of <u>being</u> one. Yet we suspect that her dreaminess was ingrained enough to have got her regarded askance in our American educational system. Was she an introverted escapist, dodging the real problems of life by resort to a private world? One must admit that, to a certain extent, she was. The fact that the story makes her a lonely child surrounded by grown-ups strengthens this conclusion. Yet though the real Alice Liddell was environed by sisters near her own age, she too, it seems, was given to this sort of escape. In the picture, for example, which shows her sisters interested in getting some grapes, she sits apparently lost in thought, with the grapes unregarded on her lap. The deep retirement of her whole mature life suggests that she made no great effort to throw herself into the stream of human intercourse, and when she at length was brought to America, she said that this trans-

Atlantic material, external world became to
her a present Wonderland.[53] Was she justified
in assuming such retirement, or did it harm
and defeat her? Who can say? Let those who
know both New York City and the Alice books choose
their own Wonderland.

Harry Morgan Ayres suggests that this un-
abashed preference for or tolerance of a dream
world is medieval.[54] Lewis Carroll is in a way
comparable with the Pearl poet or with Dante,
especially with Dante, who also immortalized
his beloved by making her the ideal experiencer
of enlightenment regarding the fantastic material
world as he understood it. Dante expressed no
doubt, however, that the ideal Beatrice was
right, real, and permanent, whereas the world

_____

53. New York Times, May 1, 1932, sec. 5, p. 7.
54. "Lewis Carroll and the 'Alice' Books,"
Columbia University Quarterly, vol. 24, pp. 158-
177 (June, 1932). The logic, the piety, the
bestiary of strange creatures, the moral considerations as in an animal fable, the moraliz-
ing of games like cards and chess, the satire on
education, the repudiation of "the world" are
characteristic medieval touches.

she left behind was a nightmare, repudiated and
foredoomed.   The modern dream is less dogmatic.
Maybe Alice _is_ the "fabulous monster,"[55] whereas
the arbitrary creatures she met are real.   Perhaps she is their dream.   At any rate, the New
York Wonderland probably thought so, agreeing with
the Unicorn.   And the extravert theory of modern
education is very unicornish.

  But Alice had other introvert traits, some
of which were less defensible.   She was timid,
as Victorian maids were supposed to be, not regarding the harm that fear can do.[56]   She was
ashamed to ask questions, lest she be thought
ignorant.[57]   She didn't like to confess, even to
herself, that she couldn't read "Jabberwocky."[58]

---

55.   _Looking-Glass,_ p. 231.   It is noteworthy
that Dante thought the world so bad and Beatrice
so good that he kept her out of the _Inferno_ and
the _Purgatorio_ as much as possible, merely there
establishing her for the stellar part in the
Paradiso.   Is the part of Sylvie in _Sylvie and
Bruno_ a sort of _Paradiso_ for Alice?
56.   _Wonderland,_ p. 19 and _passim._   See Bertrand
Russell, _Education and the Good Life,_ chap. 5.
57.   _Wonderland,_ p. 19.
58.   _Looking-Glass,_ p. 155.

She cried frequently and much.[59] She allowed
the exaltation of her dream to make her regard
the common way of life as stupid, a potentially
dangerous habit if it becomes confirmed.[60] And
though her intelligence sometimes penetrated
the fallacies of the preposterous creatures
who were browbeating her, and sometimes she
petulantly hit out in self-defense, she could
never _do_ anything effective to change her tor-
mentors or to revenge herself upon them.

It is significant also that her imagination,
the characteristic wings of escape which made
her independent of the tyrant world she could
never master, was itself largely verbal. She was
at her best in assisting with Humpty Dumpty's
exegesis of "Jabberwocky,"[61] but that very pro-

---

59. Wonderland, pp. 24, 27, 30, ff.
60. Ibid., p. 25.
61. Looking-Glass, pp. 215-217. She was proud
of knowing such words as jurors (Wonderland, p.
115), suppressed (Wonderland, p. 120), and
unsatisfactory (Looking-Glass, p. 221); but she
was ignorant of the rowing expressions to feather
and to catch a crab (Looking-Glass, p. 204),
and she sometimes made such slips as antipathies
for antipodes (Wonderland, p. 19), or the un-

cess was of a nature to make orthodox psychologists shiver, for she let the words suggest a conception of things, thus opening a way for distortion, and throwing a verbal haze between the mind and its external object of thought. The same kind of distortion is shown in her frequent puns, such as <u>tale</u> and <u>tail,</u> which influences her to remark that the narrator had reached "the fifth bend."[62] Granting that such aberrations are consciously introduced for purposes of humor, they nevertheless betray her characteristic manner of thinking. It is common observation that thing-minded, extravert people despise puns.

But of course Alice has the advantage of her word-mindedness. If she seldom thinks of people, places she has seen, or things from her

---

orthodox comparative <u>curiouser</u> <u>(Wonderland,</u> p. 26). It is true of course that all these are by way of verbal humor, but they also fit into the picture of her character.

62. <u>Wonderland,</u> pp. 39-41. The same passage plays on <u>not</u> and <u>knot.</u> Elsewhere she reflects that it will hardly take long to see the White Knight <u>off</u> <u>(Looking-Glass,</u> p. 248).

experience; her ruminations are nevertheless full of imaginary conversations, facts rather hazily learned from books or lessons, stories, poems, proverbs, jingles. Her mind rejected the idea of Mabel or Ada, whom she knew (were they counterparts of Lorina and Edith?),[63] but she welcomed and actively developed various suggestions from stories. "Then I suppose they'll soon bring the white bread and the brown?"[64] she inquired, following out the story of the Lion and the Unicorn. Her device for testing her own sanity and identity was to recite "How doth the little busy bee."[65] Thus her mind was literary, if not very practical.

---

63. Wonderland, p. 29.
64. Looking-Glass, p. 228.
65. Wonderland, p. 29. She also goes into the appropriate rimes for Humpty Dumpty (Looking-Glass, p. 209) and Tweedledum and Tweedledee (Looking-Glass, p. 181). "Father William," (Wonderland, p. 55) and " 'Tis the voice of the sluggard" (Wonderland, p. 110) are unsuccessful attempts from her repertoire. Her knowledge of facts from her school work was generally un-reliable (see Wonderland, pp. 67, 97, 103; Looking-Glass, 168). She knew the tune of the song "I give thee all, I can no more" (Looking-Glass, p. 245).

At this point it is necessary to inquire if some of these literary traits of the imaginary Alice may not have been really for the most part Lewis Carroll's traits, with which he has somewhat plentifully endowed his heroine, in spite of his effort to present a restrained and realistic picture. The character Alice was "named after a real Alice, but none the less a dream child," he wrote to Miss M. E. Manners.[66] It was the mind of Lewis Carroll, as author of the dream, that conceived the Mock Turtle, the Rocking-horse-fly, the bread-and-butter-fly, and the snap-dragon-fly,[67] conceptions in which words certainly tyrannize over things. And likewise the poems for which Alice is not represented as being responsible are nearly as derivative as the others.[68] For the fact is that, whatever

---

66. Collingwood, op. cit., p. 365.
67. Wonderland, p. 99; Looking-Glass, p. 174.
68. For example, "Beautiful Soup" is a parody on the then popular song "Star of Evening"; the White Knight's "Aged Aged Man" parodies Wordsworth's "Resolution and Independence." For a table of the obvious parodies in Lewis Carroll's books, see Williams and Madan, op. cit., p. 21.

might have been true of Alice Liddell, Lewis
Carroll had a literary mind. That is, books,
poems, stories, and information from them, were
more to him than the solid experiences of sense,
especially experiences in the adult world. As
a child he drew pictures, published an amateur
periodical, read a great deal, and excelled in
mathematics. As a man, he taught his students,
lived alone, and wrote a great many books.
Except for the children, with whom he associated
upon intimate terms, his was a life of medieval,
almost monastic retreat from society. To him
studies and children were the great realities.

His lack of much vital contact with the
adult world may account for the rigid conserva-
tism with no will for reform, which critics
have noted in him. "He could not really imagine
anything," says Chesterton, "that made the
first last and the last first."[69] Of course this
can hardly apply to the nonsense of the Alice

69. "The 100th Birthday of Nonsense," New York
Times, Jan. 24, 1932, sec. 2, pp. 1-2, 22.

books, where first and last shift with bewilder-
ing rapidity, and all the high and mighty are
only a pack of cards after all. Alice developed
from pawn to queen. Humpty Dumpty had a fall,
and the Jabberwock was slain. It was only the
actual adult world that Lewis Carroll did not seek
to reform fundamentally. Why? Probably because he was not much interested. It seemed to
be no great hardship for him to let Caesar
have the things that were Caesar's. The world
of children and the world of the literary imagination satisfied him. And his purpose of amus-
ing children made against serious social criticism. If children might find reform dull, he
was not one to put it into the story. The contrast between him and Swift or Rabelais is
not so much that he attacks abuses less mordantly,
but that he amuses children more consistently.

To understand this attitude better, we must
take into account what few writers have even
mentioned, the sexual peculiarity of the man.
A bachelor all his days, held by a strict con-

science to super-chastity, Lewis Carroll found
in a sublimated friendship with little girls the
emotional release which most men look for in
love and marriage. He did not marry, he told
Miss Manners, because he never found a woman with
whom he could imagine getting on for more than
two weeks; but with little Isa Bowman he lived
very happily for a month.[70] His letters to
children often reveal, but thinly disguised
under playful nonsense, the essential spirit of
romantic love.[71] And when the White Knight,
who, we cannot help suspecting, is in some ways
Lewis Carroll himself, takes leave of Alice,
his sentimental request that she wave her hand-
kerchief to encourage him has in it a ring of
sincerity beyond anything else in the stories.[72]
The sister's wish regarding Alice at the end of
Wonderland was that "she would keep, through
all her riper years, the simple and loving heart

---

70. Collingwood, op. cit., p. 400.
71. For example, see Moses, op. cit., pp. 251 f.
72. Looking-Glass, p. 248.

of her childhood."[73] This wish seems to contain
a mixture of religion and his characteristic
sublimated sex. If the kingdom of heaven is made
up of child-like souls, as the Bible says, then
a lover of children may expect, in the Christian
heaven, souls most especially to his taste.

In the preface to Alice Underground, the desire
for a child's love, "a little child's whispered
thanks, and the airy touch of a little child's
pure lips,"[74] is described as a motive very close
to sheer unselfishness. At any rate, it was
probably the strongest motive in Lewis Carroll's
life. The relation between sex and religion
has often been stressed.[75] It is not surpris-
ing that this less usual deviation of sex should
likewise have its religious bearing. Like the
ladies in many sonnet sequences, Alice is the
symbol of love, both romantic and religious —

---

73. Wonderland, p. 131.
74. Moses, op. cit., p. 126.
75. See William James, Varieties of Religious
Experience, passim.

alone to be accepted as "the greatest thing in
the world."

But it is the tragedy of those who build
their lives upon the love of children in this
world that the children do grow up. His own
sisters grew up, and were only a wet blanket when
he took them one day with the little Liddells
on the river. Alice grew up, and, whether or
not she kept anything of the child heart as he
wished, his letters to "My dear Mrs. Hargreaves"
hold but a pale reflection of the fresh emotion
in his letters to real children. In fact, as
one reads the life of Lewis Carroll, there rises
a growing pathos from the procession of little
girls who successively held his affections,
matured beyond his emotional reach, and left with
him at most only a sad memory of happy hours.
The brevity and futility of the often-repeated
experience remind one of the quick wilting of
cut flowers. Life is like that at best, but this
was an abbreviation of the common lot. Possibly it is his feeling of this that comes out in

his recurring use of the dream as the most fit-
ting symbol of life, especially where children
are concerned. The Looking-Glass ends with the
famous verse, "Life, what is it but a dream?"
That poem is an acrostic, spelling out the name
Alice Pleasance Liddell. Sylvie and Bruno is
introduced by the verse, "Is all our Life, then,
but a dream?" That poem is a complex acrostic
on the name Isa Bowman. Between those two
loves of Lewis Carroll had gone many others:
Alexandra (Xie) Kitchin, Isabel Standen,
Adelaide Paine, Gaynor Simpson, Gertrude Chataway
(to whom The Hunting of the Snark is inscribed),
Edith Rix, Kathleen Eschwege, Agnes Hughes,
etc.[76] Is it to be wondered at, after this experience in loving and losing, that in the poem
to Isa the dream is a gloomy one?

But the love for Alice was fresher, undimmed
by more than a vague prescience of the leave-
taking at the "brook" just ahead. The "moral"
which he apparently hoped Alice would get from

76. See Collingwood, op. cit., Chaps. 10-11.

the stories is, "Don't grow up." Here is the
object lesson in the unconscionableness of
adultdom; take heed. Behold the witless trucu-
lence of Tweedledum and Tweedledee; that is the
adult British male. Note well the Duchess, the
Queen of Hearts, the Red Queen, the White Queen;
they exemplify the adult British female. Look
at the Gryphon and the Mock Turtle; they are the
grown-up product of schools. Consider Humpty
Dumpty; he is the professor in an eggshell. And
so when she has had her experience of this sort
of thing, and with her clear wit of childhood
has pierced the shallow pretentiousness, he
hopes that his Alice will keep her child heart
through life.[77] Thus he might have Alice the
child always. It was a vain hope. He never
dared such a hope again. The "happy nightmare,"
as Chesterton calls Wonderland,[78] was a night-

---

77. See H. M. Ayres, op. cit., pp. 170-173.
Compare also the purport of Christopher Morley's
Thunder on the Left.
78. Op. cit., p. 22. Chesterton contends that
Carroll's nonsense is "nonsense for nonsense's
sake," that common sense is amputated, as Dr.

mare because it exposed the adult world which
Lewis Carroll (like a medieval monk, but for a
different motive) repudiated. It was happy because Alice, the child, was there, and he dared
to dream of her as permanently a child. The
glory of the book is the real permanence of the
"ideal Alice."

> Still she haunts me, phantomwise.
>
> Alice moving under skies
>
> Never seen by waking eyes.[79]

Jekyll amputated his conscience. But I do
not think that this amputation was just for fun,
merely "for nonsense's sake." Carroll
castigated adult common sense, slashed it and
mutilated it unmercifully, mocked it and made
merry over its dead body. He hated it. That's
why. He hated adultdom, and he scorned the adult
manner of thinking. As a philosophical logician
(some members of that calling follow the laws
of thought with no more imagination or dis-
crimination than an adding machine) he knew that
most boasted reasoning is rationalizing, conceived in pride or in self-defence after the de-
cision is made, and abounding in fallacies of
every kind. (See James Harvey Robinson, The
Mind In the Making, chap. 4.) He knew the part
that effrontery and bluff play in men's most
imposing arguments. And he knew that when an
adult lays aside the stick and begins reasoning
with a child, the change is not so great as one
might hope.
79. Looking-Glass, p. 272.

Seldom does an author make a believable character of a heroine with whom he has fallen in love. Lewis Carroll owes his success to two things. (1) By taking the point of view of Alice, he was prevented from praising her unduly and falling into the sentimentality to which, forsaking humor, he was liable. Since he hated most of the other characters, he made them disagreeable by allowing them to browbeat his heroine. (2) As for her character, he endowed her generously with his own, which, it happened, was plausibly childlike. Her self-control,[80] her truthfulness,[81] her dislike of emotional arguments,[82] her thoughtfulness,[83] her tendency to escape in dreams[84] and imagination,[85] her sensitiveness,[86] her habit of cautious

---

80. Wonderland, p. 85.
81. Ibid., p. 61.
82. Ibid., p. 65; Looking-Glass, p. 211.
83. Looking-Glass, p. 188.
84. Ibid., pp. 188-189, 272.
85. Ibid., p. 256.
86. Wonderland, pp. 55, 101-102; Looking-Glass, pp. 188, 190, 200.

understatement,[87] her embarrassment at the affection of women,[88] her sincere desire to please,[89]
her straight thinking when she really understood a situation,[90] her sincere good manners
which turned to rudeness and a desperately vehe-
ment pertness when people were too rude to her;[91]
all these traits become Alice very well, and
harmonize in her character, for they were first
genuinely fused in the character of Lewis Carroll.[92]

Many people may think that a child's character is really more simple than this. But they

---

87. "People don't fall off quite so often,
when they've had much practice." (Looking-
Glass, p. 239.) "She had never forgotten that,
if you drink much from a bottle marked 'poison,'
it is almost certain to disagree with you, sooner
or later." (Wonderland, p. 22.)
88. Wonderland, pp. 96-98; Looking-Glass, pp.
257-258.
89. Wonderland, p. 33 and passim.
90. Ibid., p. 86. What's the use of a procession if the spectators lie down and don't see it?
91. Manners: Wonderland, pp. 75, 97; rudeness:
Ibid., pp. 81, 88, 98, 125; Looking-Glass, p.
252. Probably, to children, adults seem extremely rude most of the time. Note the cross,
scolding voices or simpering, hypocritical tones
which children assume when they impersonate
adults. Are they much mistaken?
92. See Collingwood's biography, which furnishes
illustrations of these qualities on every page.

are wrong. A child's character is desperately complex, as students of childhood all know, and as all discriminating parents agree. In fact, Carroll fails to do justice to this complexity, at least to the extent of his Victorian reticences. And other people may complain that as they remember Alice of Wonderland from their early reading, she seemed a very simple child, colorless, with little or no character of her own, moving among a phantasmagoria of sharply defined individuals. Is our interpretation, sometimes between the lines, this collecting of scattered references, perhaps misleading?

Any such attribution of colorlessness to the character of Alice is probably due to: (1) the influence of Tenniel's illustrations; (2) the failure of some readers, as children, lost in a gorgeous story, to appreciate or even notice character at all; (3) the natural tendency of a fairly realistic personality to seem unremarkable among vigorous caricatures; (4) the too common assumption that any child, by virtue of

146

being a child, can as a matter of course have
no significant traits, no general interest. Most
of these obstacles to an appreciation of Alice
vanish as soon as one recognizes their existence. But the effect of the Tenniel drawings
will require some explanation.

III

Harry Furniss, who illustrated Sylvie and
Bruno, wrote that Carroll did not, in general,
like Tenniel's drawings.[93] While this statement may be colored by professional jealousy
(Carroll asked Tenniel to illustrate another
of his books[94]), there is evidence that the
illustrations, which have rivaled the popularity
of the stories themselves, were less satisfactory to the author than to the general public.

---

93. Quoted in Williams and Madan, op. cit.,
p. 250.
94. Collingwood, op. cit., p. 146. The fact
that Carroll criticized Tenniel's work while
it was in progress was doubtless only part of his
general fussy attention to details. But if one
will take the trouble to go through the references
to Tenniel in Collingwood's index, Carroll's
unfavorable comments will be found in nearly
every reference.

He complained, for one thing, that Tenniel would not work from models, and that artists who drew from their own imagination made their characters monotonously alike, or without significant individualizing traits.[95] Though this lack of individuality can hardly be urged against most of Tenniel's Wonderland creatures, it is true that his Alice has rather blank, regular features, generally suggesting too much maturity, and almost never revealing the inward appreciativeness suggested by the text. One suspects that Tenniel interpreted the various situations of Alice as if she were a grown woman, and then accommodated the postures and expressions as best he could to the scale of a child. But the worst of it is that he always presents Alice with an apparent extravert interest in her surroundings, whereas the text reveals her as busy with her own evaluations and speculations, often very skeptical of her specious companions. Carroll's photographs of Alice Liddell show a child with

_____

95. Collingwood, op. cit., p. 199.

an air of being spiritually remote from the present physical scene. Probably Tenniel, with his gift for sharp perception of those conspicuous signs which feed the cartoonist's craft, had not the temperament, the perception, or the art to draw Alice subtly with the knowing abstraction of a Mona Lisa beneath a child's simplicity. Most children, probably, would fail to appreciate such illustrations, just as they overlook the deeper implications of the story itself. Children seldom complain of a blank pretty face in a picture; they enjoy the dimpled insipidity of their dolls. They may deplore Alice's old-fashioned clothes or her long straight hair, but they hardly notice the frequent mature sophistication of her features. If she seems rather old, they attribute the impression to the length of her dress, but for most children her diminutive size is sufficient evidence of her youth. Lewis Carroll, however, may well have deplored in Tenniel's work the almost total absence of Alice Liddell's genuine

149

child nature with its piquant individual air of abstraction; and the absence or misinterpretation of his idealized Alice's inner poise and naïve, uncynical skepticism. The main trouble is that Alice is no subject for caricature. The story puts a caricatured society in very unflattering comparison with the candid intelligence of a wise but realistic child. The author was able to do both the satiric sketch and the subtly significant portrait. But Tenniel's great gift sufficed only for the sketch. His attempt at a sympathetic portrait of Alice resulted in a somewhat too graceful doll, with the expression and most of the features of an adult sophisticate. Tenniel was wise in declining to undertake illustrations for Sylvie and Bruno, a story that stressed the seriousness of Lewis Carroll, and diminished the satire.

Children often gaze intently at Tenniel's pictures while some one reads aloud the story of the Alice books. At all events, the pictures are likely to make the deeper, more immediate

impression upon them, and suggest an easy, un-
subtle interpretation of Alice's character.
Child readers hardly heed or easily forget the
heroine's revealing reveries, but remember the
doll-like figure from the drawings, quaint,
not very impressive, and somewhat irrelevant to
the astonishing creatures of wonder and satire.
When these child readers become adults, they
recall Alice as the admirable but unimportant
little spectator who won immortality by happen-
ing upon a gorgeous pageant of marvels, thanks
to the unique genius of Lewis Carroll.

But Alice was a real child without whose
unique qualities Carroll himself would never
have discovered Wonderland. And she was also a
creature of his own imagination, embodying
many of his best qualities and standing for that
which he found best in life. As such, she was
simple, candid, shrewd, a child of good will,
not to be stultified by all the bluster of imposing stupidity, immortal in her forthright and
beautiful integrity.

THE MATURE ALICE

The later life of Alice has but doubtful bearing upon her character as a child. Both
Lorina and Alice married, but Edith lived on
with their father, and died at Oxford, where she
was buried at Christ Church College. A memorial
window by Burne-Jones was dedicated to her there.
Later their father was buried near her. Lorina
became Mrs. Skene. Alice married Reginald Gervis
Hargreaves (1852-1926), a typical country
gentleman, product of Eton and Christ Church
College, Oxford. He was a good shot, a fisherman
and cricketer, a widely read man of culture,
especially in French. On his estate, called
Cufnells, near Lyndhurst in New Forest about
eighty miles from London, he cultivated a great
variety of trees, including redwoods and Douglas
pines. Here Alice lived for over forty years and
reared her three sons, two of whom, both cap-
tains, were killed in the World War. Her sur-
viving son, Captain Caryl Hargreaves, who served
through the war in the Scots Guards, later
came with her to America in 1932. At the birth
of her first son, Lewis Carroll wrote to her
under the impression that the baby was a girl
and would be named Alice. When she asked him
to be godfather to her son, he characteristically
failed to reply. (See Caryl Hargreaves, op.
cit., p. 7.) In 1891 he invited her and her husband to tea at Christ Church College. That
was the last time he saw her. He died in 1898.
(Ibid., p. 15.) Her home by the ancient New
Forest, on a low hilltop remote from the world,
was a very peaceful retreat, among rhododendrons,
with a black cat, perhaps some descendant of
Dinah, to sleep by the door. Among many pictures hung in the rooms of her house, a visitor
in 1932 saw none of Lewis Carroll or of any
subject connected with the Alice books. (See
Clair Price, "Alice Lives: in Wonderland and
in Fact," New York Times, Jan. 24, 1932, sec. 5,

p. 3.) Her husband died in 1926, leaving property
valued at £23,913, but with accumulating ex-
penses in 1928 she felt obliged to offer her
original manuscript of Alice's Adventures Underground for sale. It brought £15,400, or $75,259,
the highest price any book had ever brought in
an English auction room. A little later it was
resold with some first editions for $150,000.
(See New York Times, Jan. 24, 1932, sec. 5, p.
23: London Times, Sept. 3, 1926, p. 13, col. 4;
also Williams and Madan, op. cit., p. 111.) The
Bible and Shakespeare are the only books that
have ever rivaled these prices. In 1932 the
centenary of Lewis Carroll's birth was cele-
brated in England and in America. Alice was
then (May 24) eighty years old, but she took part
in the observances in both countries, and a
good deal was written about her. She auto-
graphed a copy of Alice in Wonderland for the
Princess Elizabeth, the only copy she is known
to have signed, though Lewis Carroll signed
a great many for his child friends, including
children of the royal family. On May 2 she was
made a Doctor of Letters at Columbia University,
with much publicity. She was feeble, and the
trip was exhausting, but on several occasions
she spoke fittingly concerning her connec-
tion with the famous book. Her son often spoke
for her in interviews. But there was something hollow about the whole celebration, for
every one realized that any actual child in the
audience was now more truly the "real Alice"
than this amiable old lady whose great fortune
it had once been to inspire the story. (See I.
Daly, "The Original Alice," Bookman, vol. 75,
pp. 164-167, May, 1932.) She was described at
this time as an elderly gray-haired lady of.
medium height, with charming old-fashioned
manners, who spoke in low tones, displayed a
quaint sense of humor, and walked with two
canes. (For portraits of her at this age, see
New York Times, Ap. 30, 1932, p. 17, col. 2;

Nov. 17, 1934, p. 15, col. 2.)   She died two
years later, Nov. 15, 1934, aged eighty-two, at
the home of her younger sister Rhoda, The
Breaches, Westerham Green, where she had lived
for some time.   The funeral was held there in
a room hung with Tenniel drawings.   She was
buried at Lyndhurst near the home where she
had spent most of her life.

BIBLIOGRAPHY

"Alice Comes to Our Wonderland." Literary Digest, vol. 113, pp. 16-17 (May 21, 1932).
About Mrs. Hargreaves' visit to New York.

Ayres, Harry Morgan. "Lewis Carroll and the 'Alice' Books." Columbia University Quarterly, vol. 24, pp. 158-177 (June, 1932).
Lecture delivered at Columbia University in honor of Alice at the time when she was given a degree. This was the celebration of the centenary of Lewis Carroll's birth. The lecture was given on May 4.

Carroll, Lewis. The Complete Works of Lewis Carroll. New York: Modern Library, n.d.
Since these are the works of Lewis Carroll, not of C. L. Dodgson, the mathematical books and other writings for adults are not included. CONTENTS: Alice's Adventures in Wonderland; Through the Looking-Glass; Sylvie and Bruno; Sylvie and Bruno Concluded; The Hunting of the Snark; Early Verse; Puzzles from Wonderland; Prologues to Plays; Phantasmagoria; College Rhymes and Notes by an Oxford Chiel; Acrostics, Inscriptions, and Other Verse; Three Sunsets and Other Poems; Stories; A Miscellany. All my references to any of these works are made with page numbers from this edition.

- - - - - -. Further Nonsense, Verse and Prose, edited by Langford Reed. New York: D. Appleton and Company, 1926.

Chesterton, G. K. "The 100th Birthday of Nonsense." New York Times, Jan. 24, 1932, sec. 2, pp. 1-2, 22.

Collingwood, Stuart Dodgson. The Life and Letters of Lewis Carroll. New York: The Century Company, 1899.
   The standard biography, by Carroll's nephew. Contains many of Carroll's letters and photographs, including several of Alice Liddell.

Daly, I. "Original Alice." Bookman, vol. 75, pp. 164-167 (May, 1932).
   A story based upon the Carroll centennial celebration. It brings out the truth that any child may be more like the real Alice of the story than was the woman that Alice became.

Hargreaves, Caryl. "Lewis Carroll as Recalled by Alice." New York Times, May 1, 1932, sec. 5, p. 7.
   Caryl Hargreaves is Alice's son, who came with her to New York in 1932. The article is accompanied by a striking Carroll photograph of Alice and her sisters.

Kingsmill, Hugh. "Lewis Carroll: A Contemporary Portrait by Fr-nk H-rr-s." Bookman, vol. 71, pp. 16-19 (March, 1930).
   An attempt, in the manner of Frank Harris, to ridicule Carroll's Victorian attitude toward. sex. There is no effort to probe Carroll's sublimations of sex.

Moses, Belle. Lewis Carroll in Wonderland and at Home, the Story of His Life. New York and London: D. Appleton and Company, 1910.
   Written for children. A little sentimental, but interesting, supplementing Collingwood at some points.

Partington, Wilfred. "The Untold Tale of Lewis Carroll." Bookman, vol. 75, pp. 78-82 (April, 1932).
   Has a few letters not in Collingwood.

BIBLIOGRAPHY (54)

Price, Clair. "Alice Lives: in Wonderland and in Fact." New York Times, Jan. 24, 1932, sec. 5, p. 3.
    Interesting account of Mrs. Hargreaves in old age at her home, Cufnells. Has a portrait showing her there.

Thompson, H. L. Article on Henry George Liddell, in Dictionary of National Biography. Supplement, vol. 3, pp. 94-96. London: Smith, Elder & Co., 1901.
    An account of the father of Alice.

Williams, Sidney Herbert and Madan, Falconer. A Handbook of the Literature of the Rev. C. L. Dodgson (Lewis Carroll). London: Oxford University Press, 1931.
    Much scholarly information about Lewis Carroll, his books, and writings about him.

Wilson, P. W. "Dodgson-Carroll: a Dual Character." New York Times, Jan. 24, 1932, sec. 5, p. 22.

Index

This index is designed to include all useful references to authors, works, subjects, etc. Merely illustrative matters and footnote references are not indexed. Materials in the illustrative essay "The Triple Personality of Alice" are not indexed. Of works that have several authors, only the first author is indexed. When a title begins with an author's name, no separate author entry is given. Numbers refer to pages.

Abbreviations in footnotes, 96
Administration, topics about, 10
Aeronautics, bibliog., 47
Agricultural Index, 47
Agriculture, bibliog., 47; topics in, 14
A.L.A. Booklist, 35
A.L.A. Index, 35
Alexander, C., *How to Locate Educational Information and Data*, 40
Allen, R. G. D., *International Trade Statistics*, 40
Allen's Synonyms and Antonyms, 43
Allibone, S. A., *Critical Dict. of Eng. Lit. and Brit. and Amer. Authors*, 55; *Poetical Quotations*, 55; *Prose Quotations*, 55
Allusions, bibliog., 54
Almanacs, 37
American Annual of Photography, 52
American Art Directory, 51
American Bibliography, 36
American College Dictionary, 42
American Historical Documents, 60
American literature, 53
American Oxford Dictionary, 42
American Women, 59
American Women Poets, 58
American Year Book, 37
Americana Annual, 37
America's Young Men, 59
Amusements, topics about, 16
Annotated Bibliography of Economic Geology, 45
Annual Bibliography of English Language and Literature, 52
Annual Magazine Subject Index, 33
Annual Register, 37
Apollo, 51
Appleton's Cyclopaedia of American Biography, 57
Architecture, bibliog, 51; topics in, 15
Arkin, H., *Statistical methods*, 79; *Tables for Statisticians*, 79
Army Almanac, 48.
Art, see Fine arts; Useful arts
Art Index, 50
Art of Scientific Investigation, 80
Astronomy, topics in, 11

Atlas of Zoögeography, 47
Atlases, Bibliog., 38; type of book, 6
Atomic energy, bibliog., 46
Audubon, J. J., *Birds of America*, 47
Authors, biographies, 58-59
Authors of Today, 59
Authors of Today and Yesterday, 58
Authors' and Printers' Dictionary, 50
Avey, A. E., *Handbook in the Hist. of Philosophy*, 39

Bacteriology, Abstracts of, 44
Bailey, L. H. *Hortus*, 47; *Standard Cyclopedia of Horticulture*, 47
Baker, E. A., *Guide to Historical Fiction*, 57; *Guide to the Best Fiction*, 57; *The History of the English Novel*, 57
Baldwin, J. M., *Dict. of Philos. and Psych.*, 39
Ballantine, J. A., *Law Dictionary*, 41
Barnes and Noble World Atlas, 38
Bartholomew, J. G., *Atlas of Zoögeography*, 47
Bartlett, J., *Familiar Quotations*, 54
Basic Reference Sources, 34
Basler, R., *Guide to Study of U.S.*, 35
Baugh, A. C., *A Lit. Hist. of England*, 53
Benét, W. R., *The Reader's Encyclopedia*, 53
Benham's Book of Quotations, 55
Bent, S. A., *Familiar Short Sayings of Great Men*, 55
Beowulf, concordance to, 56
Berry, F. A., *Handbook of Meteorology*, 46
Best Books, 35
Besterman, T., *World Bibliography...*, 41
Bibliographical Guide to English Studies, 41
Bibliographies of language and literature, 41, 52
Bibliography, type of book, 7; arrangement of, 99; list, 30-60; authority for data in, 29; how to collect list, 29; cards for, 19-29.
Bibliography and Index of Geology Exclusive of North America, 45

Bibliography of Fishes, 47
Bibliography of Meteorological Literature, 46
Bibliography of Research Studies in Education, 41
Bibliography on Public Administration, 41
Bibliotheca Americana, 36
Biography, bibliog., 57; dictionaries of, 57; topics in, 18
Biological Abstracts, 44
Biology, bibliog., 44; topics in, 13
Birds of America, 47
"Boethius To-Day," 89
Book of Authors, 59
Book of Fine Prints, 51
Book of the States, 37
Book Review Digest, 30, 35
Book reviews, how to refer to, 26
Bookman's Manual, 35
Books, bibliog., 19 guides for selecting, 34; inclusive lists, 36
Botanical Abstracts, 44
Botany, bibliog., 44; topics in, 13
Boyd, A. M., U. S. Gov't. Publications as Sources . . . for Libraries, 34
Brassy's Naval Shipping Annual, 49
Brewer, E. C., Dict. of Phrase and Fable, 53
Britannica Book of the Year, 31, 37
Britannica World Language Dictionary, 42
British Authors of the Nineteenth Century, 58
British Chemical Abstracts, 44
Browning, R., concordance, 56
Bulletins, how to refer to, 27
Business, bibliog., 40
Business Information: How to Find and Use It, 40

Cambridge History of American Literature, 53
Cambridge History of English Literature, 53
Cambridge Natural History, 46
Case study, 82
Catalogues of public documents, 34
Catholic Encyclopedia, 31
Century Cyclopedia of Names, 58
Century Dictionary and Cyclopedia, 42
Ceramic Abstracts, 51
Ceramics, bibliog., 51
Chambers' Biographical Dictionary, 58
Chambers' Encyclopedia, 31
Champion, S., Racial Proverbs, 54
Chaucer, G., concordance, 56
Chemical Abstracts, 45
Chemical Publications, 45
Chemistry, bibliog., 44; topics in, 12
Chi è?, 59
Christy, R., Proverbs, Maxims, and Phrases, 55
Chujoy, A., Dance Encyclopedia, 51
Classification of notes, 72
Coan, O. W., America in Fiction, 57
Coleridge, S. T., concordance, 56
Collier's Encyclopedia, 31
Collins, F. H., Authors' and Printers' Dictionary, 50
Collins, W., concordance, 56
Columbia Dict. of Modern European Lit., 53
Columbia Encyclopedia, 31
Columbia Lippincott Gazetteer of the World, 38

Coman, E. T., Sources of Business Information, 40
Commentary notes, 71
Commercial arts, topics in, 14
Communication, topics about, 11
Comparative method, 83
Compilation as a method, 83
Composers of Yesterday, 59
Concise Biblio. for Students of English, 41
Concise Oxford Dictionary, 42
Concordances, bibliog., 55
Condensed Chemical Dictionary, 45
Contemporary American Authors, 53
Cook, D. E., Fiction Catalog, 57; Short Story Index, 53; Standard Catalog for Pub. Libraries, 35
Cornell Conferences on Therapy, 49
Crabb, G., English Synonyms, 43
Craigie, W. A., Dict of Amer. English, 42
Critical Hist. of Eng. Lit., 55
Critical Dictionary of English Literature and British and American Authors, 55
Critical Method in Historical Research, 60
Criticism, bibliog., 55
Cross, T. P., Biblioq. Guide, 41
Cruden, A., Bible concordance, 56
Cumulative Book Index, 36; copying entry from 20, 21
Curme, G. O., English Grammar, 44
Current List of Medical Literature, 49
Cyclopedia of American Government, 41
Cyclopedia of Education, 40

Daiches, David, Critical Hist. of Eng. Lit., 55
Daniel, R. S., Professional Problems in Psychology, 39
Date, bearing on value of writing, 64
Day's Collacon, 55
Dean, B., Bibliog. of Fishes, 47
Dewey decimal system, 4, 7
Dictionaries, bibliog., 42; type of book, 6
Dictionary of American Biography, 58
Dictionary of American English 42
Dictionary of American-English Usage, 44
Dictionary of American Politics, 41
Dictionary of American Proverbs, 54
Dictionary of Americanisms . . , 44
Dictionary of Applied Chemistry, 45
Dictionary of Contemporary American Usage, 44
Dictionary of Dates, 60
Dictionary of Economics, 40
Dictionary of Modern American Usage, 44
Dictionary of Modern English Usage, 44
Dictionary of National Biography, 58
Dictionary of Philosophy and Psychology, 39
Dictionary of Phrase and Fable, 44, 53
Dictionary of Psychology, 39
Dictionary of the Bible, 39
Dictionary of the Flowering Plants and Ferns, 44
Directory of Newspapers and Periodicals, 33
Documentation, 66, 93
Documents on American Foreign Relations, 41
Dorland, W. A. N., Dorland's Illustrated Medical Dict., 50

Drama, bibliog., 56
Dramatic Index, 56
Drawing, topic about, 15

Eastman, M. H., *Index to Fairy Tales*, 57
Economics, topics in, 9
Education, bibliog., 40; topics about, 10
Education Abstracts, 40
Education Index, 40
Educational Directory, 40
Ely, J. E., *International Trade Statistics*, 40
Encyclopaedia Britannica, 31
Encyclopaedia of the Ceramic Industries, 51
Encyclopaedia of the Social Sciences, 39
Encyclopedia, type of book, 6; how to refer to, 25; list of, 31
Encyclopedia Americana, 31
Encyclopedia of American History, 60
Encyclopedia of Banking, 40
Encyclopedia of Educational Research, 40
Encyclopedia of Painting, 52
Encyclopedia of Religion and Ethics, 39
Encyclopedia of the Social Sciences, 39
Encyclopedia of World History, 60
Engineering, bibliog., 48; topics in,
Engineering Drawing, 49
Engineering Encylopedia, 49
Engineering Index, 48
Engineer's Year-Book, 48
English Grammar, 44
English language, 52
English literature, 52
English Proverbs, 55
English Synonyms, 43
Engraving, bibliog., 51; topic about, 15
Esdaile, A., *Student's Manual of Bibliography*, 53
Essay and General Literature Index, 56
Essays, bibliog., 56
Ethics, topics in, 8
Ethnology, bibliog., 45
European Composers Today, 59
Evans, C., *American Bibliography*, 36
Exhaustive Concordance to the Bible, 55
Experiment Station Record, 48
Experimental, method, 79

Fairy tales, index to, 57
Familiar Quotations, 54
Familiar Short Sayings of Great Men, 55
Fernald, J. C., *Standard Handbook of Synonyms, Antonyms and Prepositions*, 43
Fiction, bibliog., 57
Fine arts, bibliog., 50; topics in, 15
Firkins, I. T., *Index to Plays*, 56;
Footnotes, purposes, 93; when to use, 94; how to put into an essay, 95; kinds of, 96; abbreviations in, 96; explanatory, 98; original, 98
Fowler, H. W., *Dict. of Mod. Eng. Usage*, 44
French literature, 54
Funk and Wagnalls' New Standard Dictionary, 42

Gardner, E. G., *Italy*, 53
Gardner, H., *Art through the Ages*, 51
Gazetteers, 38
Genetic method, 82
Geography bibliog., 45
Geology, bibliog., 45; topics in, 12
German literature, 53

Government, bibliog., 41
Government documents, 28
Gray, T. concordance, 56
Greek literature, 54
Grove's Dict. of Music and Musicians, 51
Guide to Best Fiction, 57
Guide to Eng. Lit. from Beowulf through Chaucer and Medieval Drama, 54
Guide to Geologic Lit., 45
Guide to Historical Fiction, 57
Guide to Historical Literature, 60
Guide to Lit. of Math and Physics, 46
Guide to Lit. of Zool. Sciences, 47
Guide to Reference Books, 4, 6, 30, 34
Guide to Study of U. S., 35

Hall, T. S., *Source Book in Animal Biology*, 47
Handbook in the Hist. of Philosophy, 39
Handbook of Denominations, 39
Handbook of Greek Literature, 54
Handbook of Meteorology, 46
Harper Encyclopedia of Science, 44
Harper History of Painting, 52
Harper's Dictionary of Classical Literature and Antiquities, 60
Harris, C., *Encyclopedia of Educational Research*, 40
Harvard Dictionary of Music, 51
Harvard Guide to American History, 60
Harvard University List of Books in Psychology, 39
Hastings, James. *Dict. of the Bible*, 39;
Hawkins, R. R., *Scientific, Medical and Technical Books*, 44
Hazlitt, W. C., *English Proverbs*, 55
Henius, F., *Dict. of Foreign Trade*, 40
Herrick, R., concordance, 56
Historical Atlas, 38
Historical fiction, bibliog., 57
Historical Lights, 60
Historical method, 81
History, bibliog., 57, topics in, 17; type of book, 6
History of Architecture, 51
History of Art, 51
History of German Literature, 53
History of literature, bibliog., 53
History of Modern Colloquial English, 44
History of Modern Criticism, 55
History of the English Novel, 57
Hockett, H. C., *The Critical Method in Historical Research*, 60
Hoffman, H., *The Bookman's Manual*, 35
Home Book of Quotations, 55
Home economics, bibliog., 49
Homer, concordances, 56
Horace, concordance, 56
Hortus, 47
Hortus Second, 47
Horwill, H. W., *Dict. of Mod. Amer. Usage*, 44
How and Where to Look It Up: A Guide to Standard Sources of Information, 35
How to Locate Educational Information and Data, 40
Hoyt's New Cyclopedia of Practical Quotations, 54

Iliad, concordance, 56
Index Medicus, 50
Index of Amer. Design, 51
Index to Fairy Tales, 57
Index to Plays, 56
Index to Poetry, 57

161

Index to Short Stories, 57
Indexes, guides to, 35
Industrial arts, bibliog., 49
Industrial Arts Index, 49
Information Please Almanac, 37
Institutions, topics about, 10
International Bibliography of Historical Sciences, 60
International Cyclopedia of Music and Musicians, 52
International Cyclopedia of Prose and Poetical Quotations, 55
International Index to Periodicals, 33
International Trade Statistics, 40
Interpreter's Bible, 39
Introduction to Opera, 52
Italian Literature, 53
Italy, A Companion to Italian Studies, 53

James, G., *Mathematics Dictionary*, 46
Jane's All the World's Aircraft, 47
Jewish Encyclopedia, 31
Jones, F. D., *Engineering Encyclopedia*, 49
Journalism, bibliog., 49

Keller, H. R., *Dict. of Dates*, 60
Kelly, J., *Amer. Catalogue of Books*, 36
Kennedy, A. G., *A Concise Bibliog. for Students of Eng.*, 41
Kenyon, J. S., *American Pronunciation*, 6
Kobbe, G., *Complete Opera Book*, 51
Krapp, G. P., *The English Language in America*, 6
Kunitz, S. J., *Brit. Authors of the Nineteenth Cent.*, 58; *Twentieth Century Authors*, 58
Kurath, H., *Amer. Pronunciation*, 6

Langer, W. L., *Encyclopedia of World Hist.*, 60
Larned, J. N., *New Larned Hist. for Ready Ref.*, 60
Law, bibliog., 41; topics in, 9
Law Dictionary, 41
Leidy, W. P., *Popular Guide to Government Publications*, 34
Library classification, 4
Library of Congress cards, 22
Library of Literary Criticism, 55
Literary History of England, 53
Literary History of the United States, 54
Literary Market Place, 50
Literature, bibliog., 53-57; histories of, 53; topics about, 16
Little, C. E., *Historical Lights*, 60
Locke, A. *When Peoples Meet*, 45
Logic, topic in, 8
London Bibliog. of the Social Sciences, 40
Louttit, C. M., *Professional Problems in Psychology*, 39

Magazine articles, how to refer to, 25
Manly, H. P., *Drake's Cyclopedia of Radio and Electronics*, 50
Manual of Style, 102
Manual of the Writings in Middle English, 54
March, F. A., *Thesaurus Dict.*, 43
Mathematics, bibliog., 46; topics in, 11
Mead, P. S., *Handbook of Denominations*, 39
Medicine, bibliog., 49; topics in, 13

Mellon, M. G., *Chemical Publications*, 45
Mencken, H. L., *New Dictionary of Quotations*, 55; *The American Language*, 6
Metallurgy, bibliog., 50
Meteorology, bibliog., 46
Millett, F. B., *Contemporary Amer. Authors*, 53
Mineral Resources of the United States, 50
Mineralogy Abstracts, 46
Minerals Yearbook, 46
Mining, bibliog., 46, 50
Minto, J., *Reference Books*, 34
Modern languages, bibliog., 52
Monroe, P., *Cyclopedia of Education*, 40
Monroe, W. S., *Encyclopedia of Educational Research*, 40
Monthly Catalog of U. S. Public Documents, how to use, 28; 34
Monthly Check-list of State Publications, 34
Moulton, C. W., *Lib. of Lit. Crit.*, 55
Muir's *Atlases*, 38
Munn, G. G., *Encyclopedia of Banking*, 40
Music, bibliog., 51, 59; topics about, 16

National Cyclopedia of American Biography, 58
Natural history, bibliog., 46
Navy, bibliog, 48
Nelms, H., *Play Production*, 56
New Century Dictionary, 42
New Century Handbook of English Literature, 53
New English Dictionary on Historical Principles, 42
New International Encyclopaedia, 32
New International Year Book, 32, 37
New Larned History for Ready Reference, 60
Newman, J. R., *World of Mathematics*, 46
New Survey of Journalism, 49
New Technical Books, 49
New York Times Index, 33
Newspapers, how to refer to, 27; indexes, 33
Nicholson, M., *Dict. of American-English Usage*, 44
Nickles, J. M., *Bibliog. and Index of Geol. Exclusive of N. Amer.*, 45
Normative method, 76
Notes, classification of, 72; kinds of, 69

Opera, bibliog., 51
Organization of material for writing, 76
Orientation of a subject, 4
Otis, W. B., *Outline-Hist. of Eng. Lit.*, 53
Outline, specimens, 89; 104; how to make, 85-90; begins with essay thesis, 73
Outline notes, 69
Outline of Russian Lit., 54
Oxford Classical Dictionary, 60
Oxford Companion to Amer. Lit., 53
Oxford Companion to Classical Lit., 53
Oxford Companion to Eng. Lit., 53
Oxford Companion to French Lit., 53
Oxford Dictionary, 42
Oxford Dict. of English Proverbs, 55
Oxford History of English Lit., 54
Oxford History of Music, 52

Painting, bibliog., 52; topic about, 15
Pamphlets, how to refer to, 27
Paperbound Books in Print, 35
Paraphrase notes, 70

162

Parke, N. G., *Guide to Math. and Physics*, 46

Pearl, R. M., *Guide to Geologic Literature*, 45

Pearl, R. M., *Rocks and Minerals*, 46

Peck, H. T., *Harper's Dict. of Classical Lit. and Antiquities*, 60

People of All Nations, 46

Periodicals, lists and indexes, 32

Pharmacy, bibliog., 45

Philology, bibliog., 41; topics in, 11

Philosophers, topics about, 8

Philosophy, bibliog., 39; topics in, 7

Photography, bibliog., 52; topics about, 15

Physics, bibliog., 46; topics in, 12

Play Index, 56

Play Production, 56

Poetical Quotations, 55

Poetry, index to, 57

Political science, bibliog., 41; topics in, 9

Poole's Index to Periodical Literature, 32

Popular Guide to Govt. Publications, 34

Primary sources, 61

Printing, bibliog., 50

Professional Problems in Psychology, 39

Professions, biographies for, 59

Progress in Astronautics and Rocketry, 47

Prose Quotations, 55

Proverbs, bibliog., 54

Proverbs, Maxims, and Phrases, 55

Psychological Abstracts, 39

Psychological Index, 39

Psychology, bibliog., 39; topics in, 7

Public Administration Organizations, 41

Public Affairs Information Service Bulletin, 40

Public documents, 34

Publications of the Modern Language Association, 52

Publishing bibliog., 50.

Punctuate It Right! 102

Quarterly Cumulative Index Medicus, 50

Questionnaire method, 84

Qui Etes-vous? 59

Quotation notes, 70

Quotations, bibliog. of, 54

Racial Proverbs, 54

Radio, bibliog., 50

Radio Amateur's Handbook, 50

Radio-Television-Electronic Dictionary, 50

Reader's Adviser, 35

Reader's Encyclopedia, 53

Reader's Guide to Periodical Literature, 33

Reference Books, 34

Reference books, guides to, 34; how to refer to, 25; list, 30-60

Reinach, S., *Apollo*, 51

Religion, bibliog., 39; topics in, 8

Revision of a documented paper, 101

Rocks and Minerals, 46

Roget, P. M., *Thesaurus of Eng. Words and Phrases*, 43

Roman literature, 54

Roorbach, O. A. *Bibliotheca Americana*, 36

Rose, H. J., *Handbook of Greek Literature*, 54

Science, bibliog., 44; references on methods of, 80; topics in, 11

Science Abstracts, Physics, 46

Scope of a study, 3

Sculpture, topics about, 15

Searle, A. B., *Encyclopaedia of the Ceramic Industries*, 51

Seckler-Hudson, C., *Bibliography on Public Administration*, 41

Secondary sources, 61

Sentence outlines, 88

Serial publications, how to refer to, 27

Shaw, H., *Errors in English*, 102; *Punctuate It Right!* 102

Shepherd, W. R., *Historical Atlas*, 38

Shores, L., *Basic Reference Sources*, 34

Short stories, index to, 57

Sloan, H. S., *Dictionary of Economics*, 40

Smith, E. C., *Dictionary of Amer. Politics*, 41

Smith, R. C., *Guide to the Literature of the Zoological Sciences*, 47

Smith, W. G., *Oxford Dict. of Eng. Proverbs*, 55

Social science, topics in, 9

Sociology, bibliog., 40

Sonnenschein, W. S., *Best Books*, 35

Source footnotes, 96

Sources, evaluation of, 61

Speaker's Handbook of Epigrams and Witticisms, 55

Spiller, R. E., *Literary Hist. of the U. S.*, 54

Standard Catalog for Public Libraries, 4; 6; 35

Standard Cyclopedia of Horticulture, 47

Standard Handbook of Synonyms, Antonyms and Prepositions, 43

Standardized Plant Names, 44

Statesman's Year Book, 37

Statistical Abstracts of the U. S., 38

Statistical Methods, 79

Stevenson, B. E., *Home Book of Quotations*, 55

Strong, J., *Exhaustive Concordance to the Bible*, 56

Structure and Composition of Foods, 49

Student's Manual of Bibliography, 53

Style, Chicago Manual of, 102

Subject Index to Periodicals, 33

Subject indexes, 34

Subjects for research papers, 1-18; what to avoid in, 1-3; orientation of, 4-7; how to choose, 7; list of topics, 7-18

Subordination in outlines, 87

Summary notes, 70

Survey method, 83

Synonym dictionaries, 43

Tables for Statisticians, 79

Taylor, Archer, *Dictionary of American Proverbs*, 54

Technical Book Review Index, 35

Technical subjects, 1

Television Manual, 50

Teuffel, W. S., *Hist of Roman Lit.*, 54

Textbook of Medicine, 50

Theatre, *Who's Who in the*, 59

Thesaurus Dictionary, 43

Thesaurus of Eng. Words and Phrases, 43

Thesis for an essay, 72

Thiessen, A. H., *Weather Glossary*, 46

Thomas à Kempis, *De Imitatione Christi* concordance, 56

Thompson, O., *International Cyclopedia of Music and Musicians*, 52

Thom's Irish Who's Who, 59

Thorpe, J. F., *Dict. of Applied Chem.*, 45

Times, London, *Official Index*, 34
Title page, 22
Topics, list for research papers, 7-18
Trade, topics about, 11
Transportation, topics about, 11
Travel, topics about, 17
Trawick, B. B., *World Literature*, 54
Twentieth Century Authors, 58

Ulrich's International Periodicals Directory, 33
Union List of Serials in Libraries of the U. S. and Canada, 32
United States Catalog, Books in Print, 36
United States Government Organization Manual, 41
United States Government Publications as Sources of Information for Libraries, 34
Universal Dictionary of the English Language, 43
Universal Jewish Encyclopedia, 32
University Debaters' Annual, 41
Usage, dictionaries of, 44
Useful arts, bibliog., 47; topics in, 13

Van Nostrand's Scientific Encyclopedia, 44
Vincent, J. A., *History of Art*, 51

Walsh, W. S., *International Cyclopedia of Prose and Poetical Quotations*, 55
Warren, H. C., *Dict. of Psych.*, 39
Weather Glossary, 46
Webster's Biographical Dictionary, 58; *Dictionary of Synonyms*, 43; *Geographical Dictionary*, 38, 45; *New International Dictionary*, 43
Webster's New World Dictionary of the American Language, 54
Wellek, R., *History of Modern Criticism*, 55

Wells, J. E., *Manual of the Writings in Middle Eng.*, 54
Wer Ist's? 59
Whitaker, J., *Almanack*, 38
Who's Who, 58; other works on similar principles, 58-59
Willis, J. C., *Dict. of the Flowering Plants and Ferns*, 44
Winchell, C. M., *Guide to Reference Books*, 4, 6, 30, 34
Winton, A. L. and Winton, K. B., *Structure and Composition of Foods*, 49
World Almanac and Encyclopedia, 38
World Aviation Annual, 47
World List of Social Science Periodicals, 40
World Literature, 54
World of Mathematics, 46
Wright, C. H. C., *Hist. of French Lit.*, 54
Wright, J. K., *Aids to Geographical Research*, 45.
Writers, how to evaluate, 63
Wyld, H. C., *History of Modern Colloquial English*, 44
Wyld, H. C. K., *Universal Dict. of the Eng. Lang.*, 43

Yearbook of Food and Agricultural Statistics, 48
Yearbooks, type of books, 6; list of, 37
Year's Work in English Studies, 52
Year's Work in Modern Language Studies, 52
Young, R., Bible concordance, 56

Zesmer, D. M., *Guide to Eng. Lit. from Beowulf through Chaucer and Medieval Drama*, 54
Zigrosser, Carl, *The Book of Fine Prints*, 51
Zoölogical Record, 47
Zoölogy, bibliog., 47; topics in, 13

73 74   12 11 10 9 8 7 6 5 4 3